Berlitz®

Rom

phrase book &

Berlitz Publishing
New York   London   Singapore

Contacting the Editors
Every effort has been made to provide accurate information in this publication, but changes are inevitable. The publisher cannot be responsible for any resulting loss, inconvenience or injury. We would appreciate it if readers would call our attention to any errors or outdated information. We also welcome your suggestions; if you come across a relevant expression not in our phrase book, please contact us at: **comments@berlitzpublishing.com**

All Rights Reserved
© 2019 Apa Digital (CH) AG and Apa Publications (UK) Ltd.
Berlitz Trademark Reg. U.S. Patent Office and other countries. Marca Registrada. Used under license from Berlitz Investment Corporation.

Printed in China

Editor: Zara Sekhavati
Translation: updated by Wordbank
Cover Design: Rebeka Davies
Interior Design: Beverley Speight
Picture Researcher: Beverley Speight
Cover Photos: Shutterstock

Interior Photos: istockphoto p1, 13, 22, 25, 29, 31, 39, 43, 45, 47, 52, 54, 56, 59, 67, 69, 72, 77, 79, 80, 82, 85, 90, 93, 94 , 97, 98, 100, 106, 108, 111, 113, 114, 116, 121, 126, 129,133, 135, 139, 140, 142, 145, 146, 149, 150, 155, 157, 158, 160, 162; APA Britta Jaschinski p17, 87; APA Bev Speight p51, 172; APA A Nowitz p125

Distribution

UK, Ireland and Europe
Apa Publications (UK) Ltd
sales@insightguides.com
United States and Canada
Ingram Publisher Services
ips@ingramcontent.com
Australia and New Zealand
Woodslane
info@woodslane.com.au
Southeast Asia
Apa Publications (SN) Pte
singaporeoffice@insightguides.com

Worldwide
Apa Publications (UK) Ltd
sales@insightguides.com

Special Sales, Content Licensing, and CoPublishing
Discounts available for bulk quantities. We can create special editions, personalized jackets, and corporate imprints. sales@insightguides.com; www.insightguides.biz

Contents

Survival

Food & Drink

People

Leisure Time

Special Requirements

In an Emergency

Dictionary

Pronunciation

This section is designed to make you familiar with the sounds of Romanian using our simplified phonetic transcription. You'll find the pronunciation of the Romanian letters and sounds explained below, together with their 'imitated' equivalents. This system is used throughout the phrase book; simply read the pronunciation as if it were English, noting any special rules below. Romanian is relatively easy to read and write since it is a phonetic language in which all letters are pronounced. With the exception of â and î, all the other sounds are easy to identify with English approximations.

Consonants

Letter	Approximate Pronunciation	Symbol	Example	Pronunciation
c	1.like c in cake	c	cartofi	cartofy
	2. followed by e or i like ch in cheese	ch	ceas	cheas
			cineva	cheeneva
ch	lke k in kettle	k	chibrit	kibreet
g	1. like g in girl	g	rog	rog
	2. when followed by e or i, like g in gender	j	ginere	jeenereh
gh	like g in girl	gh	ghete	geteh
h	like h in hand	h	hartă	harter
j	like s in pleasure	zh	jucărie	zhuceree-eh
r	rolled consonant similar to the Scottish r	r	roată	rwater
s	like s in sun	s	student	stoodent
ş	like sh in short	sh	şiret	sheeret
ţ	like ts in bits	ts	ţară	tsarer

Letters b,d,f,l,m,n,p,t,v,w,x,z are generally pronounced as in English.

Vowels

Letter	Approximate Pronunciation	Symbol	Example	Pronunciation
a	like the vowel sound in cut	**a**	**alfabet**	_alfabet_
ă	lke er at the end of teacher	**er**	**masă**	_maser_
â	pronounced like **î** below; it only occurs in the middle of words	**uh**	**românește**	_romuhneshteh_
e	1. like the e in ten	**e**	**elev**	_elev_
	2. at the end of a word like the e in ten	**eh**	**carte**	_carteh_
	3. at the beginning of certain words, like ye in yes	**ye**	**este**	_yesteh_
i	1. like the e in bee	**ee**	**intrare**	_eentrareh_
	2. if unstressed at the end of a word, i is scarcely audible, softening the preceding consonant	**y**	**bani**	_ban^y_
î	there's no exact equivalent in English. Resembles the o in lesson/ kingdom	**uh**	**înțeleg**	_uhntseleg_
o	like the vowel sound in sport without pronouncing the r	**o**	**copil**	kopeel
u	like the oo in book	**oo**	**munte**	_moonteh_

Diphthongs

Letter	Approximate Pronunciation	Symbol	Example	Pronunciation
ai	like igh in high	**igh**	**mai**	*migh*
au	like ow in cow	**a⁰⁰**	**stau**	*sta⁰⁰*
ău	like o in go	**oh**	**rău**	*roh*
ea	1. no exact equivalent in English; sounds almost like a in bat	**a**	**dimineaţa**	*deemee<u>na</u>tsa*
	2. at the end of the word like aye in layer*	**eh-a**	**prea**	*preh-a*
ei	like ay in bay	**ay**	**lei**	*lay*
eu	no equivalent in English; start pronouncing the e in bed, then draw your lips together to make a brief oo sound	**e⁰⁰**	**leu**	*le⁰⁰*
ia	like ya in yard	**ya**	**iarbă**	<u>*yarber*</u>
ie	like ye in yellow	**ye**	**ieftin**	<u>*yefteen*</u>
io	like yo in yonder	**yo**	**chioşc**	*kyoshc*
iu	like ew in few	**yoo**	**iubire**	*yoo<u>beereh</u>*
oa	like wha in what	**wa**	**poate**	<u>*pwateh*</u>
oi	like oy in boy	**oy**	**doi**	*doy*
ua	like wa in watch	**wah**	**ziua**	<u>*zee-wa*</u>
uă	similar to ue in influence	**wer**	**două**	<u>*do*</u>*-wer*

***Hyphens are sometimes inserted between sounds to avoid confusion.**

How to use this Book

Sometimes you see two alternatives separated by a slash. Choose the one that's right for your situation.

ESSENTIAL

I'm on vacation/business.

Sunt în vacanţă/Am venit în interes de serviciu. *soont uhn vacantser/am veneet uhn eenteres deh serveechee-oo*

I'm going to...

Merg la/Cu destinaţia spre... *merg la/coo desteenatsya spreh*

I'm staying at the...Hotel.

O să stau la hotelul... *o ser sta⁰⁰ la hotelool...*

Words you may see are shown in YOU MAY SEE boxes.

YOU MAY SEE...

LA VAMĂ	customs
BUNURI SCUTITE DE TAXE VAMALE	duty-free goods
BUNURI DE DECLARAT	goods to declare

Any of the words or phrases listed can be plugged into the sentence below.

Tickets

When's...to Paris?

La ce oră pleacă... spre Paris? *la cheh orer pleh-acer... spreh Paris*

the (first) bus

autobuz *aootobooz*

the (next) flight

zbor *zbor*

the (last) train

Tren regio *tren rejee-o*

Romanian phrases appear in purple.

Read the simplified pronunciation as if it were English. For more on pronunciation, see page 7.

The Dating Game

Are you on Facebook/Twitter?
Ai cont pe Facebook/Twitter?
igh cont peh Facebook/Twitter

Can I join you?
Pot să te însoțesc? *pot ser teh uhnsotsesc*

You're very attractive.
Ești foarte atrăgător _m_/atrăgătoare _f_.
yeshty fwarteh atrergertor/atrergertwareh

For Communications, see page 48.

Related phrases can be found by going to the page number indicated.

When different gender forms apply, the masculine form is followed by _m_; feminine by _f_

When addressing people, you need to use **Domnul** for Mr. and **Doamna** for Mrs., followed by the person's surname.

Information boxes contain relevant country, culture and language tips.

Expressions you may hear are shown in You May Hear boxes.

YOU MAY HEAR...

Vorbesc doar puțin engleza.
vorbesc dwar pootseen engleza

I only speak a little English.

Color-coded side bars identify each section of the book.

Survival

ESSENTIAL

I'm on vacation/business.	**Sunt în vacanţă/Am venit în interes de serviciu.** *soont uhn vacantser/am veneet uhn eenteres deh serveechee-oo*
I'm going to…	**Merg la/Cu destinaţia spre…** *merg la/coo desteenatsya spreh*
I'm staying at the…Hotel.	**O să stau la hotelul…** *o ser staoo la hotelool…*

YOU MAY HEAR…

Paşaportul, vă rog. *pashaportool, ver rog*	Your passport, please.
Care este scopul vizitei dumneavoastră? *careh yesteh scopool vizitay doomnewastrer*	What's the purpose of your visit?
Unde locuiţi? *oondehlocooeetsy*	Where are you staying?
Cât doriţi să staţi? *cuht doreetsy ser statsy*	How long are staying?
Cu cine aţi venit? *coo cheeneh atsy veneet*	Who are you here with?

Border Control

I'm just passing through.	**Sunt în trecere doar.**
	soont uhn trechereh dwar
I'd like to declare...	**Doresc să declar...**
	doresc ser declar...
I have nothing to declare.	**Nu am nimic de declarat.**
	noo am neemeec de declarat

YOU MAY HEAR...

Aveți ceva de declarat? — Anything to declare?
avetsy chehvah deh declarat

Trebuie să plătiți vamă pentru acest obiect. You must pay duty.
trebooyeh ser plerteetsy vamer pentroo achest obyect

Vă rog să deschideți acest sac. — Open this bag.
ver rog ser deskeedetsy achest sac

YOU MAY SEE...

LA VAMĂ	customs
BUNURI SCUTITE DE TAXE VAMALE	duty-free goods
BUNURI DE DECLARAT	goods to declare
NIMIC DE DECLARAT	nothing to declare
GHIȘEUL DE PAȘAPOARTE	passport control
POLIȚIA	police

Money

ESSENTIAL

Where's...?	**Unde se află...?** <u>oon</u>deh seh <u>a</u>fler...
the ATM	**bancomatul** banco<u>ma</u>tool
the bank	**o bancă** o <u>ban</u>cer
the currency	**birou de schimb**
exchange office	<u>beero</u>-ool deh skeemb
When does the bank	**Când se deschide/închide banca?**
open/close?	<u>Cuhnd</u> seh des<u>kee</u>deh/uhn<u>kee</u>deh <u>ban</u>ca
I'd like to change	**Aş dori să schimb dolari/lire sterline în lei.**
pounds dollars/	Ash do<u>ree</u> ser skeemb do<u>lar</u>/<u>lee</u>reh sterleeneh uhn <u>ley</u>
sterling into Lei.	
I'd like to cash.	**Acceptaţi cecuri de voiaj?**
traveler's cheques	acchep<u>tats</u>y che<u>coo</u>ry deh vo-<u>yazh</u>

15

The import and export of Romanian currency is prohibited, but there is no restriction on the amount of foreign currency visitors can bring into the country. Foreign currency can be changed at airports, banks, most hotels and currency exchange offices in major cities. Avoid changing a large amount of money unless you think you will spend it, as you may not easily be able to change it back. Never change money with street dealers.

At the Bank

I'd like to change money/get a cash advance.	**Aş dori să schimb bani/să scot în avans.** *ash doree ser skeemb bany/ser scot uhn avans.*
What's the exchange rate/fee?	**Care este cursul/rata de schimb valutar?** *careh yesteh coorsool/rata deh scheemb valootar*
I think there's a mistake.	**Cred că s-a făcut o greşeală.** *cred cer s-a fercoot o greshealer*
I lost my traveler's cheques.	**Mi-am pierdut cecurile de voiaj.** *Meeam pierdoot chehcooreeleh deh voyazh*
My card...	**Cardul meu...** *cardool me⁰⁰...*
was lost	**s-a pierdut** *s-a pyerdoot*
was stolen	**mi s-a furat...** *mee sa foorat*
doesn't work	**nu funcţionează...** *noo foonctsyonazer*
The ATM ate my card.	**Bancomatul nu mi-a returnat cardul.** *Bancomatool noo meea retoornat cardool*

For Numbers, see page 166.

Banks are open from Monday to Friday between 8:30a.m. and 6:00p.m. Some also open on Saturday between 9:00a.m. and 1:00p.m.
Foreign currency can be changed at airports, banks and in most hotels, but exchange bureaus will generally offer the best rate.
At some banks, cash can be obtained from ATMs with Visa™, Eurocard™, American Express® and many other international cards. Instructions are often given in English. Banks with a change sign will exchange foreign currency. You can also change money at travel agencies and hotels, but the rate will not be as good. Remember to bring your passport when you want to change money.

YOU MAY SEE...

INTRODUCEŢI CARDUL AICI	insert card here
ANULEZ	cancel
ŞTERGERE	clear
INTRODUCEŢI PIN-UL	enter PIN
RETRAGERE	withdrawal
DIN CONTUL CURENT	from checking [current] account
DIN CONTUL DE ECONOMII	from savings account
CHITANŢĂ	receipt

YOU MAY SEE...

Romania's currency is **Leu** (plural **Lei** *lay*), abbreviated to **RON**.

Notes: 1, 5, 10, 50, 100 and 500 **lei** *lay*

Coins: 1, 5, 10 and 50 **bani** *bahnee*

1 leu = 100 bani

Getting Around

ESSENTIAL

How do I get to town?	**Cum să ajung în oraş?**	_coom_ ser _azhoong_ uhn _orash_
Where's...?	**Unde este...?**	_oondeh_ _yesteh_
the airport	**aeroportul**	_aeroportool_
the train station	**gara**	_gara_
the bus station	**staţia de autobuz**	_statsya_ deh _aootobooz_
the subway [underground] station	**staţia de metrou**	_statsyeh_ deh _metrooo_
Is it far from here?	**Este departe de aici?**	_yesteh_ departeh deh _aeechy_
Where do I buy a ticket?	**Unde pot să-mi cumpăr un bilet?**	_oondeh_ pot _sermy_ coomper oon _beelet_
A one-way/return-trip ticket to...	**(bilet) dus/dus-întors pentru...**	_(beelet)_ doos/doos-uh_ntors_ pentroo
How much?	**Cât costă?**	_cuht_ coster
Which gate/line?	**De la care poartă/linie?**	_Deh la_ _careh_ _pwar_ter/_leeneeeh_
Which platform?	**De la ce peron?**	_deh la cheh_ peron
Where can I get a taxi?	**De unde pot lua taxi?**	deh _oondeh_ pot loo-_a_ _taxee_
Take me to this address.	**Vreau să merg la adresa aceasta.**	_vra^oo_ ser merg la _adresa_ _acha_sta
Can I have a map?	**Îmi puteţi da o hartă?**	uhm_y_ _pootets_y da o _harter_

Tickets

When's...to Paris?	**La ce oră pleacă... spre Paris?**	la cheh _orer_ pleh-acer... spreh _Paris_
the (first) bus	**(primul) autobuz**	_(preemool)_ aootobooz

the (next) flight	**(următorul) zbor** *(oormertorool) zbor*
the (last) train	**(ultimul) tren regio** *(oolteemool) tren rejee-o*
Where do I buy a ticket?	**De unde pot cumpăra un bilet?** *deh oondeh pot coomperah oon beelet*
One/Two ticket(s) please.	**Un/Două bilet(e), vă rog.** *oon/dohooer beelet/beeleteh, ver rog*
For today/tomorrow.	**azi/mâine** *azy/muhyneh*
A . . . ticket.	**Un bilet** *oon beelet*
one-way	**numai dus** *noomigh doos*
return trip	**dus-întors** *doos-uhntors*
first class	**clasa întâi** *clasa uhntuhy*
business class	**business class** *business class*
economy class	**clasa a doua** *clasa a dowa*
How much?	**Cât costă?** *cuht coster*
Is there a discount for . . . ?	**Există o reducere pentru . . . ?** *egzeester oh rehdoochehreh pentroo . . .*
children	**copii** *copeey*
students	**studenți** *stoodentsy*
senior citizens	**persoane în vârstă** *pehrswaneh uhn vuhrster*
tourists	**turişti** *tooreeshty*
The express bus/train, please.	**Autobuzul expres/Trenul inter-city, vă rog.** *aootoboozool ekspres/trenool inter-city, ver rog*
The local bus/train, please.	**Autobuzul local/Trenul regio, vă rog.** *aootoboozool local/trenool rejee-o, ver rog*
I have an e-ticket.	**Am un bilet electronic.** *am oon beelet electroneec*
Can I buy a ticket on the bus/train?	**Pot cumpăra un bilet în autobuz/tren?** *pot coomperra oon beelet uhn aootobooz/tren*
Do I have to stamp the ticket before boarding?	**Trebuie să compostez biletul înainte de îmbarcare?** *trebooye ser compostez beeletool uhnaheenteh deh uhmbarcareh*

How long is this ticket valid?	**Cât timp este valabil acest bilet?**
	cuht teemp yesteh vala*beel* *achest* bee*let*
Can I return on the same ticket?	**Pot să mă întorc utilizând acelaşi bilet?**
	poht ser mer uhn*torc* *ooteeleezuhnd* *ache*lash bee*let*
I'd like to...	**Aş vrea să... rezervarea.**
my reservation.	*ash vreh-a ser rezer*vareh*-a*
cancel	**anulez** *anoo*lez
change	**schimb** *skeemb*
confirm	**confirm** *con*feerm

For Days, see page 168.

For Time, see page 168.

Plane

Airport Transfer

How much is a taxi to the airport?	**Cât costă un taxi până la aeroport?**
	cuht *coster* oon ta*xee* puhner lah aero*port*
To...Airport, please.	**La aeroport..., vă rog.** *la aero*port*..., ver rog*
My airline is...	**Compania mea aeriană este...**
	*compa*neea *meh-a aehree*aner *yes*teh...
My flight leaves at...	**Avionul meu decolează la...**
	*avee*onool *meh*oo*deco*leh*-a*zer la...
I'm in a rush.	**Mă grăbesc.** *mer grer*behsc
Can you take an alternate route?	**Puteţi să o luaţi pe un alt traseu?**
	*pootets*y ser o *looats*y peh oon alt tra*se*oo
Can you drive faster/slower?	**Puteţi conduce mai repede/încet, vă rog?**
	*pootets*y con*doo*cheh migh *repe*deh/uhn*chet* ver rog

Checking In

Where's check-in?	**Unde se face înregistrarea?**
	oondeh se *fa*cheh uhnrehgeestrareh-a
My name is...	**Mă numesc...** *mer noo*mesc

The Romanian international airport **Otopeni** is situated 18km from the centre of Bucharest. A regular bus service links the airport to the centre and there is also an excellent taxi service. Allow plenty of time for the journey to and from the airport, as this is a very busy route and there are frequent traffic jams.

YOU MAY HEAR...

Cu ce companie aeriană zburaţi?
coo cheh companee-eh a-ehreeaner zburatsy

Internă sau internaţională?
eenterner saoo eenternatsyonaler

La care terminal? *la careh termeenal*

What airline are you flying?

Domestic or international?

What terminal?

YOU MAY SEE...

SOSIRI	arrivals
PLECĂRI	departures
BAGAJE	baggage claim
SECURITATE	security
ZBORURI INTERNE	domestic flights
ZBORURI INTERNAŢIONALE	international flights
ÎNREGISTRARE	check-in
ÎNREGISTRARE BILETE ELECTRONICE	e-ticket check-in
PORŢI DE PLECARE	departure gates

I'm going to…	**Cu destinaţia…** *coo desteenatseea…*
I have…	**Eu am…** *eoo am*
one suitcase	**o valiză** *oh vahleezer*
two suitcases	**două valize** *do-wer vahleezeh*
one piece	**o bucată** *oh boocater*
How much luggage is allowed?	**Câte bagaje sunt permise?** *cuhte bagazheh soont permeeseh*
Is that pounds or kilos?	**În livre sau kilograme?** *uhn leevreh sao kilogrameh*
Which terminal?	**La care terminal?** *la careh termeenal*
Which gate?	**La care poartă?** *la careh pwarter*
I'd like a window/ an aisle seat.	**un loc la fereastră/un loc spre culoar** *oon loc la ferastrer/oon loc spreh coolwar*
When do we leave/arrive?	**La ce oră plecăm/ajungem?** *lah cheh orer plecerm/azhoonjehm*
Is the flight delayed?	**Are întârziere zborul?** *areh uhntuhrzee-ereh zborool*
How late?	**Ce întârziere are?** *cheh uhntuhrzee-ehreh areh*

Luggage

| Where is/are…? | **Unde se află/sunt …?** *oondeh seh afler/soont* |
| the luggage trolleys | **cărucioarele** *cerroochwareleh* |

YOU MAY HEAR...

Următorul! oormer*torool*

Pașaportul/biletul, vă rog.
pashaportool, beeletool ver rog

Doriți să înregistrați bagaje?
doreetsy ser uhnregeestratsy bagazheh

Acesta este prea mare pentru un bagaj de mână. *achestah yesteh preh-a mareh pentroo uhn bagazh deh muhner*

Dumneavoastră v-ați împachetat aceste bagaje? *Doomnewastrer vahtsy uhnmpaketat achesteh bagazheh*

V-a dat cineva ceva să transportați?
vah daht cheenevah ser transpohrtatsy

Scoateți-vă pantofii din picioare.
scwatehtsyver pantohfeey deen peec'wareh

Acum are loc îmbarcarea...
acoom areh loc uhmbarcareh-a...

Next!

Your passport/ticket, please.

Are you checking any luggage?

That's too large for a carry-on carry-on [hand luggage].

Did you pack these bags yourself?

Did anyone give you anything to carry?

Take off your shoes.

Now boarding...

the luggage lockers	**cabinele de bagaje** *cabeeneleh deh bagazheh*
the baggage claim	**zona de ridicare a bagajelor** *zona deh reedeecareh a bagazhehlor*
My luggage has been lost/stolen.	**Bagajele mele au fost rătăcite/furate.** *bagazheleh meleh aoo fost rertercheeteh/foorateh*
My suitcase is damaged.	**Geamantanul meu este deteriorat.** *jeh-amantanool meu yesteh detereeorat*

Finding your Way

| Where is/are...? | **Unde este...?** _oondeh yesteh_ |
| the currency exchange | **biroul de schimb** _beero-ool deh skeemb_ |

> Baggage porters are available at the airport only. Luggage trolleys can be found at the airport as well as at Central Bucharest Railway Station (**Gara de Nord**). Don't hesitate to ask a taxi driver to help you with your bags.

the car hire	**închirieri auto** _uhnkeereeyery aooto_
the exit	**ieşire** _yeshireh_
the taxis	**taxi** _taxee_
Is there... into town?	**Există...spre oraş?** _egzeester... spreh orash_
a bus	**autobuz** _aootobooz_
a train	**tren** _tren_
a metro [subway]	**metrou** _metrooo_

Train

Where's the station?	**Unde este gara?** _oondeh yesteh garah_
How far is it?	**Este departe până la...?** _yesteh departeh puhner la..._
Where is/are...?	**Unde este...?** _oondeh yesteh_
the ticket office	**casa de bilete** _casa deh beeleteh_
the information desk	**biroul de informaţii** _beero-ool deh informatseey_
the luggage lockers	**cabinele de bagaje** _cabeeneleh deh bagazheh_
the platform	**peronul** _peronool_

Can I have a schedule [timetable]?	**Îmi puteţi da un mers al trenurilor?** *uhmi pootets^y da oon mers al trenooreelor*
How long is the trip?	**Cât durează călătoria?** *cuht dooreh-azer cerlertoreea*
Is it a direct train?	**Este un tren direct?** *yesteh oon tren deerect*
Do I have to change trains?	**Trebuie să schimb trenurile?** *trebooyeh ser skimb trenooreeleh*
Is the train on time?	**Ajunge la timp trenul?** *azhoonjeh la timp trenool*

For Asking Directions, see page 33.

For Tickets, see page 18.

YOU MAY SEE...

PEROANE	platforms
BIROU DE INFORMAŢI	information
REZERVĂRI	reservations
SALA DE AŞTEPTARE	waiting room
SOSIRI	arrivals
PLECĂRI	departures

Departures

Which track [platform] to...?	**Care este linia/peronul pentru...?** *Careh yesteh leeneea/peronool pentroo...*
Is this the [platform]/train to...?	**Aceasta este linia trenului pentru...?** *Achasta yesteh leeneea trenoolui pentroo...*
Where is [platform]...?	**Unde este linia/peronul...?** *Oondeh yesteh leeneea/peronool...*
Where do I change for...?	**Unde să schimb pentru...?** *Oondeh ser skimb pentroo...*

On Board

Can I sit here/open the window?	**Pot sta aici?** *pot sta a-eechy*
That's my seat.	**Acesta este locul meu.** *Achesta yesteh locool me°°.*
Here's my reservation.	**Am o rezervare.** *am o rezervareh*

Bus

Where's the bus station?	**Unde este stația de autobuz?** *Oondeh yesteh statsya deh aootobooz?*
How far is it?	**Ce distanță este până acolo?** *cheh deestantser yesteh puhner acolo*

YOU MAY HEAR...

Biletele, vă rog. *beeletehle ver rog*	Tickets, please.
Trebuie să schimbați la... *Trebooyeh ser skimbatsy la...*	You have to change at...
Următoarea oprire... *Oormertwareh-a opreereh...*	Next stop...

How do I get to...?	**Cum să ajung la...?** *coom ser azhoong la...*
Is this the bus to...?	**Acesta este autobuzul către...?**
	Achesta yesteh aᵒᵒtoboozool certreh...?
Can you tell me when to get off?	**Puteţi să-mi spuneţi când trebuie să cobor?** *pootetsʸ sermʸ spoonetsʸ cuhnd trebooyeh ser cobor*
Do I have to change buses?	**Trebuie să schimb autobuzul?** *trebooyeh ser skeemb aᵒᵒtoboozool*
Stop here, please!	**Vă rog, opriţi aici.** *ver rog opreetsʸ a-eechʸ*

For Tickets, see page 18.

Metro

Where's the metro station?	**Unde este staţia de metrou?** *Oondeh yesteh statsya de metroᵒᵒ.*
A map, please.	**O hartă, vă rog.** *O harter, ver rog.*
Which line for...?	**Care este linia pentru...?** *Careh yesteh leenya pentroo...?*

YOU MAY SEE...

STAŢIE DE AUTOBUZ	bus stop
SOLICITARE OPRIRE	request stop
INTRARE/IEŞIRE	entrance/exit
COMPOSTAŢI-VĂ BILETUL	stamp your ticket

Which direction?	**Ce direcţie?** *cheh deerectsee-eh*
Do I have to transfer [change]?	**Trebuie să schimb?** *treboo-yeh ser skeemb*
Is this the metro to...?	**Acesta este metroul către?** *Achesta yesteh metro-ool certreh*

How many stops to...? **Câte staţii sunt până la...?**
Cuhteh statseey soont puhner la...

Where are we? **Unde suntem?** *Oondeh soontem*

For Tickets, see page 18.

Boat & Ferry

When is the ferry to...? **La ce oră este feribotul către...?**
La cheh orer yesteh fereebotool certreh...

Can I take my car? **Pot să îmi iau maşina?**
Pot ser uhmy yaoo masheena

What time is the next sailing? **La ce oră este următoarea plecare în larg?**
La cheh orer yesteh oormertwareh-a plecareh uhn larg

Can I book a seat/cabin? **Pot să rezerv un loc/o cabină?**
Pot ser rezerv oon loc/oh cabiner

How long is the crossing? **Cât timp durează traversarea?**
cuht teemp dooreh-azer traversareh-a

For Finding your Way, see page 24.

YOU MAY SEE...

COLAC DE SALVARE/ BARCĂ DE SALVARE	life boats
VESTĂ DE SALVARE	life jacket

Taxi

Where can I get a taxi? **De unde pot lua un taxi?**
deh oondeh pot lwa oon taxee

Can you send a taxi? **Puteţi să -mi comandaţi un taxi, vă rog?**
pootetsy sermy comandatsy oon taxee ver rog

Do you have number for a taxi? **Aveţi un număr de taxi?**
Avetsy oon noomer de taxee

I'd like a taxi now/for	**Aş dori un taxi acum/pentru mâine la ora...**
tomorrow at...	*Ash doree oon taxee acoom/pentroo muhyneh la orah...*
Pick me up at...	**Veniţi să mă luaţi la...** *Veneetsy ser mer lwatsy la...*
I'm going to...	**Cu destinaţia...** *Coo desteenatseea...*
this address	**adresa aceasta** *adresa achasta*
the airport	**aeroport** *a-eroport*
the train station	**gară** *garer*
I'm late.	**Sunt în întârziere.** *Soont uhn uhntuhrzyereh*
Can you drive	**Aţi putea să conduceţi mai repede/încet?**
faster/slower?	*atsy pooteh-a ser condoochetsy migh rehpehdeh/uhnchet*
Stop/Wait here.	**Puteţi să mă aşteptaţi.** *pootetsy ser mer ashteptatsy*
How much?	**Cât costă?** *cuht coster*
You said it would cost..	**Aţi spus că va costa...** *Atsy spoos cer vah costah...*
Keep the change.	**Păstraţi restul.** *perstratsy restool*

Bicycle & Motorbike

I'd like to hire...	**Aş vrea să închiriez...** *ash vreh-a ser uhnkeeree-ez*
a bicycle	**o bicicletă.** *o beecheecleter*
a moped	**o motoretă** *o motoreter*
a motorcycle	**o motocicletă/un scuter** *o motocheecleter/oon scooter*
How much per	**Cât costă locaţia pe zi/săptămână?**
day/week?	*cuht coster locatsee-a peh zee/serptermuhner*

YOU MAY HEAR...

Unde doriţi? _oondeh doreets_ᵧ
Care este adresa? _careh yesteh adresa_
Se aplică o taxă de noapte/pentru aeroport.
seh apleecer o taxer deh nwapteh/
pentroo a-eroport

Where to?
What's the address?
There's a nighttime/
airport surcharge.

Metered vehicles, both state owned (**GETAX**) and private, are
available in Bucharest and all larger towns and are an inexpensive
means of travel. Taxi drivers can issue a receipt for the fare on request.
It is customary to give a tip in addition to the amount shown on the
meter. Taxis are easily identified by a light on top of the vehicle.

Can I have a helmet/lock?	**Îmi puteţi da o cască/încuietoare?** _uhmi pootets_ᵧ _da o cascer/uhncooyetwareh_
I have a puncture/ flat tyre.	**Am o pană.** am o paner

Car

Car Hire

Where's the car hire?	**Unde este biroul de închirieri auto?** _oondeh yesteh beero-ool deh uhnkeeree a_ᵒᵒ_to_
I'd like...	**Aş dori...** ash doree
a cheap/small car	**o maşină ieftină/mică** o masheener yefteener/meecer
an automatic/ a manual	**cu cutie automată/manuală** coo cootee-eh aootomater/manwaler

air conditioning	**aer condiţionat**	*aer conditsyonat*
a car seat	**scaun pentru copil**	*scaoon pentroo copeel*
How much...?	**Cât costă?**	*cuht coster*
per day/week	**pe zi/săptămână**	*pe/zee serptermerner*
per kilometer	**pe kilometru**	*pe kilometroo*
for unlimited mileage	**pentru un număr nelimitat de kilometri** *pentroo oon noomer neleemeetat deh kilometree*	
with insurance	**cu asigurare**	*coo aseegoorareh*
Are there any discounts?	**Oferiţi şi reduceri?**	*ofereetsy shee redoochehry*

Most roads are not very wide but the major routes are reasonably well maintained. There are no motorways except for a short toll motorway between Bucharest and Pitesti. Traffic regulations are similar to any Western European country, with priority given to vehicles coming from the right at main junctions. It is customary to give a short signal on your horn when overtaking. Aside from the motorway, roads do not have phone facilities in case of an accident.

Fuel Station

Where's the fuel station?	**Unde este cea mai apropiată stație de benzină?** *oondeh yesteh cha migh apropee-ater statsee-eh deh benzeener*
Fill it up.	**Faceți plinul, vă rog.** *fachetsy pleenool ver rog*
. . .euros, please.	**. . .euro, vă rog.** *eh-ooroh, ver rog*
I'll pay in cash/by credit card.	**Pot plăti cu această carte de credit?** *pot plertee coo achaster carteh deh credeet*

For Numbers, see page 166.

YOU MAY HEAR...

Aveți permis de conducere internațional? *Avetsy permees deh condoochehreh internatsyonal*	Do you have an international driver's license?
Pașaportul, vă rog. *Pashaportool ver rog*	Your passport, please.
Am nevoie de un avans. *Am nevoyeh deh oon avans*	I'll need a deposit.
Vă rog să semnați în locul acesta. *Ver rog ser semnatsy uhn locool achesta*	Initial/Sign here.

There are car rental facilities at the airport and in major cities. The main rental offices are the National Tourist Office (**ONT**) and the Romanian Automobile Club (**ACR**). To hire a car you must be over 21 and have held a full driving licence for more than one year. Your hotel can help you with further information, or contact the **ONT**.

Asking Directions

Is this the way to…?	**Acesta este drumul către…?**
	achesta yesteh droomool certreh…
How far is it to…?	**Ce distanţă este până la…?**
	cheh deestantser yesteh puhner la…
Where's…?	**Unde se află …?** *oondeh seh afler*
…Street	**… strada** *stradah*
this address	**adresa aceasta** *adresa achasta*
the highway	**autostrada** *aºº tostrada*
[motorway]	

YOU MAY SEE…

BENZINĂ	gas [petrol]
FĂRĂ PLUMB	unleaded
NORMALĂ	regular
SUPER	super
MOTORINĂ	diesel

Can you show me on the map?	**Puteţi să-mi arătaţi pe hartă unde sunt?**
	pootetsy sermy arertatsy peh harter oondeh soont
I'm lost.	**M-am rătăcit.** *mam rertercheet*

Parking

Can I park here?	**Pot să parchez aici?** *Pot ser parkez a-eechy*
Is there a garage near here?	**Este vreun Service prin apropiere?**
	yesteh vreººn servees preen apropee-ereh
Where's…?	**Unde este …?** *Oonde yesteh…*
the parking lot [car park]	**parcarea** *parcareah*
the parking meter	**parcometrul** *parcometrool*

YOU MAY HEAR...

drept înainte *drept uhn<u>aee</u>nteh*	straight ahead
stânga <u>*stuhn*</u>*gah*	left
dreapta *dreh-aptah*	right
după colţ *dooper <u>colts</u>*	around the corner
vis-à-vis *veez-a-<u>vee</u>*	opposite
înapoi; în spate *uhnap<u>oy</u>; uhn <u>spat</u>eh*	behind
lângă <u>*luhn*</u>*ger*	next to
după <u>*dup*</u>*er*	after
nord/sud *nord, sood*	north/south
est/vest *est/vest*	east/west
la semafor *la sema<u>for</u>*	at the traffic light
la intersecţie *la inter<u>sec</u>tsyeh*	at the intersection

How much...?	**Cât costă?** *cuht <u>cos</u>ter*
per hour	**pe oră** *peh <u>or</u>er*
per day	**pe zi** *peh <u>zee</u>*
for overnight	**pe noapte** *peh nw<u>ap</u>teh*

Breakdown & Repair

My car broke down/ won't start.	**Maşina mea are o pană de motor.** *ma<u>shee</u>na meh-a <u>a</u>reh o <u>pa</u>ner deh mo<u>tor</u>*
Can you fix it (today)?	**Puteţi să o reparaţi (azi)?** *poo<u>tets</u>y ser oh repa<u>rats</u>y az^y*
When will it be ready?	**Când va fi gata?** *cuhnd va fee <u>ga</u>ta*
How much?	**Cât costă?** *cuht <u>cos</u>ter*

YOU MAY SEE...

	STOP	stop
	CEDEAZĂ TRECEREA	yield
	PARCAREA INTERZISĂ	no parking
	SENS UNIC	one way
	ACCESUL INTERZIS	no entry
	ACCESUL VEHICULELOR ESTE INTERZIS	no vehicles allowed
	DEPĂȘIREA INTERZISĂ	no passing
	URMEAZĂ UN SEMAFOR	traffic signal ahead
	IEȘIRE	exit

Accidents

There was an accident. **A fost un accident.** *a fost oon accheedent*

Call an ambulance/ the police. **Chemați un doctor/poliția.** *kematsy oon doctor/poleetsee-a*

Places to Stay

ESSENTIAL

Can you recommend a hotel?	**Puteţi să-mi recomandaţi un hotel?** *pootets*y *serm*y *recoman*dats*y oon hotel*
I made a reservation.	**Am o rezervare.** *am o rezer*vareh*
My name is...	**Mă numesc ...** *mer noo*mesc*...
Do you have a room...?	**Aveţi o cameră...?...** *a*vets*y oh camerer*
for one/two	**pentru o persoană/două persoane** *pen*troo o per*swaner*/*do*-wer per*swaneh*
with a bathroom	**cu baie** *coo* bayeh*
with air conditioning	**cu aer condiţionat** *coo* a*-er condeetsee-o*nat*
For...	**Pentru...** *Pen*troo...*
Tonight	**O noapte** *O* nwapteh*
two nights	**două nopţi** *do*-wer nopts*y*
one week	**o săptămână** *o serptermuhner*
How much?	**Cât costă?** *cuht* coster*
Is there anything cheaper?	**Aveţi ceva mai ieftin?** *a*vets*y*cheva migh* yefteen*
When's check-out?	**Când trebuie eliberată camera?** *Cuhnd* trebooye eleebe*hrater* camera*
Can I leave this in the safe?	**Pot să las asta în seif?** *Pot ser las* asta uhn* seif*
Can I leave my bags?	**Pot să îmi las bagajele?** *Pot ser uhm*y *las ba*gazheleh*
The bill please.	**Nota de plată, vă rog!** *nota deh* plater *ver rog*
Can I have a receipt?	**Puteţi să-mi daţi, vă rog, o chitanţă?** *poo*tets*y *serm*y *dats*y *ver rog o kee*tantser*
I'll pay in cash/ by credit card.	**Voi plăti cu numerar/card de credit.** *Voi pler*tee *coo noome*rar*/card deh* credeet*

It is advisable to book accomodation in advance if you intend to visit Romania during the peak season. However, there are a variety of options on offer:

Large hotels tend to cater to business travelers or to package tours that cover the Black Sea resorts, spa towns or cities linked with the life of Count Dracula. There are also an increasing number of motels in Romania, catering specifically for the motorist.

The so-called '**Agroturisme**' offers private accommodation in the country, and is becoming increasingly popular for the clean rooms and home-cooked meals.

Cabane, a network of chalets for hikers in the mountains, offer mostly basic, cheap and friendly accommodation. You will find them listed in the official **Cabane Turistice** map.

Somewhere to Stay

Can you recommend…?	**Îmi puteţi recomanda…?** *Uhmy pootetsy recomandah…*
a hotel	**un hotel** *oon hotel*
a hostel	**un hostel** *oon hostel*
a campsite	**un loc de campare** *oon loc deh campareh*
a bed and breakfast (B&B)	**pentru cazare şi micul dejun** *pentroo cazareh shee meecool dezhoon*
What is it near?	**Ce se află în apropiere?** *Cheh seh afler uhn apropiereh*
How do I get there?	**Cum să ajung acolo?** *coom ser ajung acolo*

Hotels in Romania are classified from five-star to one-star, or de luxe. Few hotels offer full- or half-board. Upon arrival at a hotel you'll be asked to fill in a registration form (**formular**).

For an indication of what to expect, most rooms in three-star hotels have en-suite bathrooms and toilets. In two-star and one-star hotels, the bathroom and toilet may be shared, and visitors are advised to bring their own essentials, like soap and toilet paper. Breakfast is usually included in the price, but it is still advisable to query this in lower category and cheaper hotels.

Please note, it is unwise to leave valuables in hotel rooms of any category in Romania.

At the Hotel

I have a reservation.	**Am o rezervare.**	*am o rezervareh*
My name is...	**Mă numesc ...**	*mer noomesc*
Do you have a room...?	**Aveţi o cameră...?**	*avetsy o camerer...*
with a	**cu toaletă/duş**	
toilet/shower	*coo twaleteleh /doo-sh*	
with air conditioning	**cu aer condiţionat**	*coo a-er condeetsee-onat*
that's smoking/	**pentru fumători/nefumători**	
non-smoking	*pentroo fumertory/nefumertory*	
For...	**Pentru...**	*Pentroo*
tonight	**o noapte**	*o nwapteh*
two nights	**două nopţi**	*do-wer noptsy*
a week	**o săptămână**	*o serptermuhner*
Do you have...?	**Aveţi...?**	*Avetsy...*
a computer	**un computer**	*oon compyooter*
an elevator [a lift]	**lift**	*leeft*

(wireless) internet service	**Internet wireless** *eenter<u>net</u> wireless*
room service	**servicii la cameră** *serveechee^y la <u>ca</u>merer*
a pool	**piscină** *pees-<u>chee</u>ner*
a gym	**sală de sport** *<u>sa</u>ler deh sport*
I need...	**Am nevoie de...** *am ne<u>voy</u>eh deh...*
an extra bed	**un pat suplimentar** *oon <u>pat</u> soopleemen<u>tar</u>*
a cot	**un pătuţ pentru copil** *oon per<u>toots</u> pentroo co<u>peel</u>*
a crib	**un pătuţ pentru copil** *oon per<u>toots</u> pentroo co<u>peel</u>*

For Numbers, see page 166.

YOU MAY HEAR...

Paşaportul/cardul de credit, vă rog.	Your passport/credit card, please.
<u>Pasha</u>portool/cardool deh <u>cre</u>deet ver rog	
Completaţi acest formular.	Fill out this form.
Completats^y a<u>che</u>st formoolar	
Vă rog să semnati în locul acesta.	Sign here.
Ver rog ser sem<u>nats</u>^y uhn <u>lo</u>cool a<u>che</u>sta	

Price

How much per night/week?	**Cât costă pe noapte/săptămână?** *cuht coster peh nwapte/serptermuhner*
Does that include breakfast/tax?	**Sunt incluse şi micul dejun şi taxele?** *soont inclooseh shee meecool dezhoon shee taxeleh*
Are there any discounts?	**Oferiţi şi reduceri?** *ofereetsy shee redoochery*

Preferences

Can I see the room?	**Pot să văd camera?** *pot ser verd camera*
I'd like a...room.	**Aş dori o cameră...** *ash doree o camerer...*
better	**mai bună** *migh booner*
bigger	**mai mare** *migh mareh*
cheaper	**mai ieftină** *migh yefteener*
quieter	**mai liniştită** *migh leeneeshteet*
I'll take it.	**O iau.** *o yaoo*
No, I won't take it.	**Nu-mi place.** *noomy placheh*

Questions

Where is/are...?	**Spuneţi-mi unde se află...?** *spoonetseemy oondeh se afler...*
the bar	**barul** *barool*
the bathrooms	**băile** *bereeleh*
the elevator [lift]	**liftul** *leeftool*
Can I have...	**Îmi puteţi da** *Uhmi pootetsy da*
a blanket	**o pătură** *o pertoorer*
an iron	**un fier de călcat** *oon fier deh cerlcat*
the room	**camera** *camerah*
key/key card	**o cheie/cartelă de acces** *o keyeh/carteler deh akches*
a pillow	**o pernă** *o perner*
soap	**un săpun** *oon serpoon*

toilet paper	**hârtie igienică** *huhrtyeh eegee-ehneecer*
a towel	**un prosop** *oon prosop*
Do you have an adapter for this?	**Aveți un adaptor pentru asta?** *avetsy oon adaptor pentroo asta*
How do you turn on the lights?	**Cum se aprind luminile?** *coom seh apreend loomeeneeleh*
Can you wake me at…?	**Puteți să mă treziți la ora…, vă rog?** *pootetsy ser mer trezeetsy la ora…, ver rog*
Can I leave this in the safe?	**Pot să las asta în seif?** *Pot ser las asta uhn seif* *pot ser las asta uhn seif*
Can I have my things from the safe?	**Îmi puteți da lucrurile din seif?** *uhmi pootetsy da loocrooreeleh deen seif*
Is there mail/a message for me?	**Am vreun mesaj?** *am vreh-oon mesazh*
Do you have a laundry service?	**Aveți serviciu de spălătorie?** *avetsy serveechyoo deh sperlertoree-eh*

YOU MAY SEE…

TRAGEȚI/ÎMPINGEȚI	push/pull
BAIE	bathroom [toilet]
DUȘURI	showers
LIFT	elevator [lift]
SCĂRI	stairs
AUTOMATE PENTRU BĂUTURI ȘI ALIMENTE	vending machines
GHEAȚĂ	ice
SPĂLĂTORIE	laundry
NU DERANJAȚI	do not disturb
UȘĂ DE INCENDIU	fire door
IEȘIRE DE INCENDIU	(emergency) exit
APEL DE TREZIRE	wake-up call

Problems

There's a problem.	**Am o problemă.** _am o problemer_
I lost my key/key card.	**Mi-am pierdut cheia/cartela.**
	meeam pee-pyehrdoot keya/cartela
I've locked my key/	**Mi-am uitat cheia/cartela în cameră.**
key card in the room.	_myam ooitat keyah/cartelah uhn camerer_
There's no hot water/	**Nu este apă caldă/hârtie igienică.**
toilet paper.	_noo yesteh aper calder /huhrtee-eh eejee-eneecer_
The room is dirty.	**Camera este murdară.** _camerah yesteh moordarer_
There are bugs in	**Sunt gândaci în cameră.**
the room.	_soont guhndachy uhn camehrer_
the air	**aerul condiţionat**
conditioning	_aerool condeetsyonat_
the fan	**ventilatorul** _venteelatorool_
the heat [heating]	**încălzirea** _uhncerlzeereh-a_
the light	**lumina** _loominah_
the TV	**televizorul** _televeezorool_
the toilet	**toaleta** _twaleteh_
...doesn't work.	**... nu funcţionează.** _...noo foonctsyoneh-azer_
Can you fix...?	**Puteţi repara...?** _pootetsy repara..._
I'd like another room.	**Aş dori o altă cameră.**
	ash doree o alter camerer

Unlike the U.S., most of Europe runs on 220-volt electricity, and plugs are two-pronged. You may need a converter and/or an adapter for your appliance.

Checking Out

When's check-out?	**Când trebuie eliberată camera?**
	cuhnd trebooyeh eleeberater camerah
Can I leave my	**Pot să îmi las bagajele aici până când…?**
bags here until…?	*pot ser-my las bagazheleh aeechy puhner cuhnd…*
Can I have an itemized	**Puteţi să-mi daţi, vă rog, o chitanţă?**
bill/a receipt?	*pootetsy sermy datsy ver rog o keetantser*
I think there's a	**Cred că s-a făcut o greşeală.**
mistake.	*cred cer sah fercoot o greshealer*
I'll pay in cash/	**Voi plăti cu numerar/carte de credit.**
by credit card.	*voi plertee coo noomerar/carteh deh credeet*

Renting

I reserved an	**Am rezervat un apartament/o cameră.**
apartment/a room.	*am rezervat oon apartament/o camerer*
My name is…	**Mă numesc…** *mer noomesc*
Can I have the keys?	**Îmi daţi vă rog cheile?** *uhmy datsy ver rog ke-eeleh*
Are there…?	**Există …?** *egzeester*
dishes	**veselă** *veseler*
pillows	**perne** *perneh*
sheets	**cearşafuri** *che-arshe-afoory*
towels	**prosoape** *proswapeh*

kitchen utensils	**ustensile de bucătărie** *oostenseeleh deh boocerteree-eh*	
When do I put out the bins/recycling?	**Când trebuie să duc afară coşul de gunoi/ obiectele reciclabile?** *cuhnd trebooyeh ser dooc afarer coshool deh goonoy*	
...is broken.	**este defect.** *yesteh defect*	
How does... work?	**Cum funcţionează...?** *coom foonctsyoneh-azer*	
the air conditioner	**aparatul de aer condiţionat** *aparatool deh aer condeetsyonat*	
the dishwasher	**maşina de spălat vase** *masheenah deh sperlat vaseh*	
the freezer	**congelatorul** *condjelatorool*	
the heater	**sistemul de încălzire** *seestemool deh uhncerlzeereh*	
the microwave	**cuptorul cu microunde** *cooptorool coo meecro-oondeh*	
the refrigerator	**frigiderul** *freegeedehrool*	
the stove	**aragazul** *aragazool*	
the washing machine	**maşina de spălat** *masheenah deh sperlat*	

Cameră mobilată or rented accommodation in private flats and houses is increasingly available to visitors. Details can be found at the local tourist office; otherwise taxi drivers can be a useful source of information.

Domestic Items

I need...	**Am nevoie de...** *am nevoyeh deh...*	
an adapter	**un adaptor** *oon adaptor*	
aluminum foil	**folie de aluminiu** *folee-eh deh aloomeenyoo*	
a bottle opener	**un deschizător de sticle** *oon deskeezertor deh steecleh*	

a broom	**o mătură** *o mertoorer*
a can opener	**un deschizător de conserve** *oon deskeezertor deh conserveh*
cleaning supplies	**articole de curăţenie** *arteecoleh deh coorertsenyeh*
a corkscrew	**un tirbuşon** *oon terbooshon*
detergent	**detergent** *detergent*
dishwashing liquid	**lichid de spălat vase** *leekeed deh sperlat vaseh*
bin bags	**saci pentru gunoi** *sachy pentroo goonoy*
a lightbulb	**un bec** *oon bec*
matches	**nişte chibrituri** *neeshteh keebreetoory*
a mop	**un mop** *oon mop*
napkins	**nişte şerveţele** *neeshteh shervetsele*
paper towels	**prosoape de hârtie** *proswapeh deh huhrteeyeh*
plastic wrap [cling film]	**folie de plastic** *folee-eh deh plasteec*
a plunger	**un desfundător pentru scurgere** *oon desfoondertor pentroo scoorjereh*
scissors	**o foarfecă** *o fwarfecer*
a vacuum cleaner	**un aspirator** *oon aspeerator*

For In the Kitchen, see page 85

At the Hostel

Is there a bed available?	**Aveţi un pat liber?**	*Avetsy oon pat leeber*
I'd like...	**Aş vrea ...**	*ash vreh-a*
a single/double room	**o cameră cu un pat/două paturi**	*o camerer coo oon pat/do-wer patoory*
a blanket	**o pătură**	*o pertoorer*
a pillow	**o pernă**	*o pe-rner*
sheets	**cearşeafuri**	*cheh-arshe-afoory*
a towel	**un prosop**	*oon prosop*
Do you have lockers?	**Aveţi dulapuri?**	*Avetsy doolapoory*
When do you lock up?	**La ce oră este închiderea?**	*La cheh orer yesteh uhnkeedehreh-a*
Do I need a membership card?	**Am nevoie de un card de membru?**	*Am nevoyeh deh oon card deh membroo*
Here's my international student card.	**Acesta este cardul meu internaţional de student.**	*Achesta yesteh cardool meoo eenternatsyonal deh stoodent*

Cămin de studenţi or youth hotels, are run by the student travel service, **CTT**, can be found in most major towns. They tend to give priority bookings to large groups and are open only in July and August. They can be booked directly when you are there and they are an inexpensive accomodation option.

Going Camping

Can I camp here?	**Pot să campez aici?**	*Pot ser campez aeechy*
Where's the campsite?	**Unde este locul de campare?**	*Oondeh yesteh locool deh campareh*
What is the charge per day/week?	**Cât costă locaţia pe zi/săptămână?**	*Cuht coster locatsee-a peh zee/serptermuhner*

Are there…?	**Există …?** *egzeeste*
cooking facilities	**spaţii pentru gătit** *spatsee{}^y pentroo gerteet*
electric outlets	**prize** *preezeh*
laundry facilities	**spaţii pentru spălat rufe**
	spatsee{}^y pentroo sperlat roofeh
showers	**duşuri** *dooshoor{}^y*
tents for hire	**corturi de închiriat** *cortoor{}^y deh uhnkiree-at*
Where can I empty	**Unde pot să golesc toaleta ecologică?**
the chemical toilet?	*Oondeh pot ser golesc twaletah ecolojeecer*

For Domestic Items, see page 44.

Camping facilities of a standard acceptable to foreign visitors are almost non-existent in Romania. However, you can obtain a list of designated campsites from Romanian National Tourist Offices.

YOU MAY SEE…

APĂ POTABILĂ	drinking water
CAMPAREA INTERZISĂ	no camping
FOCURILE/GRĂTARELE SUNT INTERZISE	no fires/barbecues

Communications

ESSENTIAL

Where's an Internet-Cafe?	**Unde se află pe aici un internet cafe?** *Oondeh seh afler pe aeetchy uhn eenternet cafe*
Can I access the internet/check my e-mail?	**Pot să accesez Internetul/să îmi verific e-mail-ul?** *Pot ser akchesehz eeternetool ser uhmy vereefeec ee-maylool*
How much per half hour/hour?	**Cât costă o jumătate de oră/o oră de folosire?** *cuht coster o joomertateh deh orer/ o orer deh foloseere*
How do I connect/ log on?	**Cum să mă conectez?** *Coom ser mer mer conectez*
A phone card, please.	**O cartelă de telefon, vă rog.** *O carteler deh telefon, ver rog*
Can I have your phone number?	**Îmi spuneți vă rog numărul dumneavoastră de telefon?** *Uhmy spoonetsy ver rog noomerool doomneh-avwastrer deh telefon*
Here's my number/ e-mail.	**Acesta este numărul/e-mail-ul meu.** *Achesta yesteh noomerool/ee-maylool meºº*
Call me.	**Sunați-mă.** *Soonatseemer*
E-mail me.	**Trimiteți-mi un e-mail.** *Treemeetetseemy oon ee-mayl*
Hello. This is...	**Alo, ... la telefon.** *alo ... la telefon*
Can I speak to...?	**Aș vrea să vorbesc cu ...** *ash vreh-a ser vorbesc coo*
Can you repeat that?	**Repetați vă rog?** *Repetatsy ver rog*
I'll call back later.	**O să sun mai târziu.** *O ser soon may tuhrzeeoo*
Bye.	**La revedere.** *la revedereh*
Where's the post office?	**Unde este poșta?** *Oondeh yesteh poshta*
I'd like to send this to...	**Aș dori să trimit asta la...** *Ash doree ser treemeet astah la...*

Online

Where's an internet cafe?	**Unde se află pe aici un Internet-Cafe?** _oondeh seh afler pe aeechy uhn eenternet cafe_
Does it have wireless internet?	**Are Internet wireless?** _are eenternet wireless_
What is the WiFi password?	**Care este parola pentru WiFi?** _care yesteh parolah pentroo Wee-Fee_
Is the WiFi free?	**Este gratuit WiFi-ul?** _yesteh gratooeet Wee-Fee-ool_
Do you have bluetooth?	**Aveţi Bluetooth?** _avetsy Bluetooth_
Can you show me how to turn on/off the computer?	**Îmi puteţi arăta cum să pornesc/opresc computerul?** _uhmy pootetsy arerta coom ser pornesc/ opresc compyooterool_
Can I...?	**Pot să...** _pot ser..._
access the internet	**accesez Internetul** _akchesez eenternetool_
check my e-mail	**verific e-mail-ul** _vereefeec ee-maylool_
print	**imprim** _eempreem_
plug in/charge my laptop/iPhone/ iPad/BlackBerry?	**conectez/încarc laptopul/iPhone-ul/iPad-ul/BlackBerry-ul?** _conectez/uhncarc laptopool, iPhoneool/iPadool/BlackBerryool_
access Skype?	**accesez Skype-ul?** _akchesez Skype-ool_
How much per half hour/hour?	**Cât costă o jumătate de oră/o oră de folosire?** _cuht coster o joomertateh deh orer/ o orer deh foloseere_
How do I...?	**Cum să (mă)...?** _coom ser (mer)_
connect/ disconnect	**conectez/deconectez** _conectez/deconectez_
log on/off	**conectez/deconectez** _conectez/deconectez_
type this symbol	**tastez acest simbol** _tastez achest seembol_
What's your e-mail?	**Care este e-mail-ul dumneavoastră?** _careh yesteh ee-maylool doomneh-avwastrer_
My e-mail is...	**E-mail-ul meu este...** _ee-maylool meoo yesteh..._
Do you have a scanner?	**Aveţi un scaner?** _avetsy oon scanner_

Social Media

Are you on Facebook/ Twitter?	**Ai cont pe Facebook/Twitter?** _Ay cont peh Facebook/Twitter_
What's your user name?	**Care este numele tău de utilizator?** _Careh yesteh noomeleh teroo deh ooteeleezator_
I'll add you as a friend.	**Te voi adăuga ca prieten.** _Teh voi aderoogah ca pree-ehten_
I'll follow you on Twitter.	**Te voi urmări pe Twitter.** _Teh voi oormeree peh Twitter_
Are you following...?	**Umărești...?...?** _Oormereshtʸ..._

YOU MAY SEE...

ÎNCHIDE	close
ȘTERGERE	delete
E-MAIL	e-mail
IEȘIRE	exit
AJUTOR	help
MESAGERIE INSTANT	instant messenger
INTERNET	internet
CONECTARE	log in
(MESAJ)NOU	new (message)
PORNIT/OPRIT	on/off
DESCHIS	open
IMPRIMARE	print
SALVARE	save
TRIMITERE	send
UTILIZATOR/PAROLĂ	username/password
INTERNET WIRELESS	wireless internet

I'll put the pictures on Facebook/Twitter.
Voi publica fotografiile pe Facebook/Twitter.
Voy poobleeca fotografee-eeleh pe Facebook/Twitter

I'll tag you in the pictures.
Te voi eticheta în fotografii.
Teh voy eteeketah uhn fotografeey

Phone

A phone card/prepaid phone, please.
O cartelă de telefon, vă rog.
O carteler deh telefon ver rog

How much?
Cât costă? *cuht coster*

Where's the pay phone?
Unde este telefonul public?
Oondeh yesteh telefonool pooblic

What's the area country code for...?
Care este prefixul pentru...?
Careh yesteh prefeexool pentroo

What's the number for Information?
Care este numărul pentru Informaţii?
Careh yesteh noomerool pentroo informatseey

I'd like the number for...
Aş dori numărul pentru...
Ash doree noomerool pentroo...

I'd like to call collect [reverse the charges].
Aş vrea să telefonez cu taxă inversă.
ash vreh-a ser telefonez coo taxer eenverser

My phone doesn't work here.
Telefonul meu nu funcţionează aici.
Telefonool meoo noo foonctsyoneh-azer aeechy

What network are you on?	**În ce reţea sunteţi dumneavoastră?** *Uhn cheh retseh-a soontetsy doomneh-avwastrer*
Is it 3G?	**Este cumva 3G?** *yesteh coomvah 3Geh*
I have run out of credit/minutes.	**Nu mai am credit/minute.** *Noo migh am credeet/meenooteh*
Can I buy some credit?	**Aş putea cumpăra credit?** *Ash pooteh-a coomperah credeet*
Do you have a phone charger?	**Aveţi un încărcător de telefon?** *Avetsy oon uhncercertor deh telefon*
Can I have your number?	**Îmi puteţi spune numărul dumneavoastră de telefon?** *Uhmi pootetsy spooneh noomer-rool doomneh-avwastrer deh telefon*
Here's my number.	**Acesta este numărul meu.** *Acestah yesteh noomer-rool meoo*
Please call/text me.	**Vă rog să mă sunaţi/să imi trimiteţi un SMS.** *Ver rog ser mer soonatsy/ser unmy treemeetetsy oon SMS*
I'll call/text you.	**Vă voi suna/trimite un SMS.** *Ver voy soona/treemeeteh oon SMS*

For Numbers, see page 166.

YOU MAY HEAR...

Cine e la telefon? *Chineh ye la telefon*
Who's calling?

Aşteptati, vă rog. *Ashteptatsy ver rog*
Hold on.

Vi-l/V-o dau la telefon.
Veel/Voh daoo la telefon
I'll put you through to him/her.

Nu este aici/vorbeşte pe altă linie.
Noo yesteh aeechy/ vorbeshteh peh alter leenye
He/She is not here/on another line.

Doriţi să lăsaţi un mesaj?
Doreetsy ser lersatsy oon mesazh
Would you like to leave a message?

Sunaţi mai târziu/în zece minute.
Soonatsy migh tuhrzeeoo/uhn zeche meenooteh
Call back later/in ten minutes.

Poate să vă sune el/ea?
Pwateh ser ver sooneh yel/ya
Can he/she call you back?

Care este numărul dumneavoastră de telefon? *Careh yesteh noomerool doomneh-avwastrer deh telefon*
What's your number?

Telephone Etiquette

Hello. This is...	**Alo, ... la telefon.**	*alo ... la telefon*
Can I speak to...?	**Aş vrea să vorbesc cu ...**	*ash vreh-a ser vorbesc coo*
Extension...	**Interior ...**	*eenteree-or*
Speak louder/more slowly, please.	**Vorbiţi mai tare/încet, vă rog.**	*vorbeetsy migh tareh/uhnchet ver rog*
Can you repeat that?	**Puteţi repeta, vă rog?**	*pootetsy repetah ver rog*
I'll call back later.	**Vă voi suna mai târziu.**	*ver voy soona migh tuhrzeey*
Bye.	**La revedere**	*la revedereh*

Fax

Can I send/receive a fax here?	**Pot trimite/primi un fax aici?**
	Pot treemeeteh/preemee oon fax a-eechy?
What's the fax number?	**Care este numărul de fax?**
	Care yesteh noomerool deh fax?
Please fax this to…	**Vă rog să trimiteţi asta prin fax la…**
	Ver rog ser treemeetetsy asta preen fax la…

Post

Where's the post office/mailbox?	**Unde este poşta/cutia poştală?**
	Oondeh yesteh poshta/cootee-ya poshtaler?
A stamp for this postcard/letter to…	**Un timbru pentru această carte poştală/scrisoare către…** *Oon teembroo pentroo achaster carteh poshtaler/scrisware certreh…*
How much?	**Cât costă?** *cuht coster*
Send this package by airmail/express.	**Trimiteţi acest colet par avion/prin poşta rapidă.**
	Treemeetetsy achest colet par avion/poshta rapeeder.
A receipt, please.	**O chitanţă, vă rog.** *O keetantser ver rog.*

YOU MAY HEAR...

Completaţi formularul de declaraţie
vamală. *Completatsy formoolarool deh*
declaratsyeh vamaler

Fill out the customs
declaration form.

Care este valoarea?
Careh yesteh valwareah

What's the value?

Ce este înăuntru?
Cheh yesteh uhneroontroo

What's the value?

The sign **PTTR** indicates a post office in Romania. Post offices
provide telegram and telephone facilities as well as postal
services. They do not usually have fax facilities. Opening hours are
generally from 8:00a.m. to 6:00p.m. Post boxes are yellow and some
have a separate box for local mail only (**loco**). Stamps can also be
purchased from tobacconists and hotel reception desks.

Food & Drink

Eating Out

ESSENTIAL

Can you recommend a good restaurant/bar?	**Îmi puteți recomanda un restaurant/bar bun?** *uhm*ʸ *pootets*ʸ *recoman*d*a oon resta*ᵒᵒ*rant/bar boon*
Is there a traditional/ an inexpensive restaurant nearby?	**Există vreun restaurant tradițional/nu prea scump prin apropiere?** *egzeester vreh-oon resta*ᵒᵒ*rant traditsional/noo preh-a scoomp preen apropee-ereh*
A table for..., please.	**Putem avea o masă...?** *pootem aveh-a o maser*
Can we sit...?	**Putem sta...?** *pootem sta*
here/there	**aici/acolo?** *a-eech*ʸ*/acolo*
outside	**afară** *afarer*
in a non-smoking area	**într-o zonă pentru nefumători** *uhntroh zoner pentroo nefoomertor*ʸ
I'm waiting for someone.	**Aștept pe cineva.** *Ashtept peh cheeneva.*
Where are the toilets?	**Unde este toaleta?** *oondeh yesteh twaleta*
The menu, please.	**Meniul, vă rog.** *menee-ool ver rog*
What do you recommend?	**Ce ne recomandați?** *cheh neh recoman*d*ats*ʸ
I'd like...	**Aș vrea ...** *ash vreh-a*
Some more..., please.	**Mai vreau puțin ..., vă rog.** *migh vreh-a*ᵒᵒ *pootseen,...ver rog*
Enjoy your meal!	**Poftă bună!** *Pofter booner*
The check [bill], please	**Nota de plată, vă rog.** *Notah deh plater, ver rog*
Is service included?	**Serviciul este inclus?** *serveechyool yesteh eencloos*
Can I pay by credit card/have a receipt?	**Pot plăti cu această carte de credit?** *pot plertee coo achaster carteh deh credeet*

Where to Eat

Can you recommend...?	**Puteți recomanda ...?** *pootets*^y *recomanda*
a restaurant	**un restaurant** *oon resta⁰⁰rant*
a bar	**un bar** *oon bar*
a café	**o cafenea** *oh cafeneh-a*
a fast food place	**un local fast-food** *oon local fast-food*
a cheap restaurant	**un restaurant ieftin** *oon resta⁰⁰rant yefteen*
an expensive restaurant	**un restaurant scump** *oon resta⁰⁰rant scoomp*
a restaurant with a good view	**un restaurant cu o vedere frumoasă** *oon resta⁰⁰rant coo o vedereh froomwaser*
an authentic/a non-touristy restaurant	**un restaurant autentic/non-turistic** *oon resta⁰⁰rant aootenteec/non-tooreesteec*

Romania offers a variety of places where you can eat and drink, ranging from simple snack bars to luxury restaurants. Most restaurants still display the category markings I, II and III; the higher the category, the higher the price you can expect to pay. Many of the larger hotels have a category I restaurant, although most restaurants usually offer one or more set menus which provide a good meal at a fair price. **Han** are large, moderately priced restaurants, usually with rustic decor. Some have Romanian folk music entertainment in the evening. For traditional Romanian fare at inexpensive prices, you will also find **Autoservire** (self-service restaurants), **bufet** (small restaurants found in railway stations), and the **Bufet expres** — stand-up cafeterias for quick meals of rather limited choice.

Reservations & Preferences

I'd like to reserve a table…	**Doresc să rezerv o măsă pentru...** *doresc ser rezerv o maser pentroo*
for two	**două persoane.** *do-wer perswaneh*
for this evening	**seara aceasta** *seh-ara aceastah*
for tomorrow at…	**mâine la ora...** *muhyneh lah orah*
A table for two, please.	**O masă pentru două persoane, vă rog.** *o maser pentroo do-wer perswaneh, ver rog*
I have a reservation.	**Am o rezervare.** *am o rezervareh*
My name is…	**Mă numesc...** *mer noomesc*
Could we have a table..?	**Putem avea o masă ...?** *pootem aveh-a o maser*
here/there	**aici/acolo** *a-eechy/acolo*
on the terrace	**pe terasă** *peh teraser*
outside	**afară** *afarer*
in a non-smoking area	**în zona de nefumători** *uhn zona deh nefoomertory*
in the corner	**în colţ** *uhn colts*
by the window	**lângă fereastră** *luhnger fereh-astrer*
in the shade	**la umbră** *la oombrer*
in the sun	**la soare** *la swareh*
Where are the toilets?	**Unde este toaleta?** *oondeh yesteh twaleta*

YOU MAY HEAR...

Aveți rezervare? _avetsy rezervare_	Do you have a reservation?
Câte persoane? _cuhteh perswaneh_	How many?
Fumător sau nefumător? _foomertor saoo nefoomertor_	Smoking or non-smoking?
Sunteți gata (să comandați)? _soontetsy gata (ser comandatsy)_	Are you ready (to order)?
Ce doriți? _cheh doreetsy_	What would you like?
Vă recomand... _ver recomand..._	I recommend...
Poftă bună! _pofter booner_	Enjoy your meal.

How to Order

Excuse me, sir/ma'am?	**Pardon** _pardon_
We're ready (to order)	**Suntem gata (să comandăm).** _soontem gata (ser comanderm)_
The wine list, please.	**Lista de vinuri, vă rog.** _leesta deh veenoory ver rog_
I'd like...	**Aș vrea ...** _ash vreh-a_
a bottle of...	**o sticlă de** _o steecler deh_
a carafe of...	**o carafă de...** _o carafer deh_
a glass of...	**un pahar de** _oon pahar deh_
The menu, please.	**Meniul, vă rog.** _menee-ool ver rog_
Do you have...?	**Aveți ...?** _avetsy..._
a menu in English	**un meniu în engleză** _oon meneeoo uhn englezer_
a fixed price menu	**un meniu cu prețuri fixe** _oon meneeoo coo pretsury feexeh_
a children's menu	**un meniu pentru copii** _oon meneeoo pentroo copeey_
What do you recommend?	**Ce ne recomandați?** _cheh neh recomandatsy_
What's this?	**Ce este aceasta?** _cheh yesteh achasta_

What's in it?	**Ce conține?**	_cheh_ contseeneh
Is it spicy?	**Este picantă?**	_yesteh_ peecanter
Without…, please.	**Fără…, vă rog.**	_ferrer…, ver rog_
I'd like some more.	**Mai vreau puțin.**	migh vreh-aoo pootseen
Can I have more …, please?	**Puteți să îmi mai dați puțin…, vă rog?**	pootetsy ser uhmy migh datsy pootseen … ver rog
Just a small portion.	**Numai puțin.**	noomigh pootseen
Nothing more, thanks.	**Nimic altceva, mulțumesc.**	neemeec altcheva multsoomesc
It's to go [take away].	**De luat acasă.**	deh lwat acaser

Note that some dishes may be priced by weight (per 100 grammes, for example), and you should therefore expect a final price more expensive than that listed on the menu.
For meals without a garnish, you should specify your desired side dish or the waiter may choose this for you.
If the restaurant has run out of a dish, it may be crossed out on the menu or simply appear without a price. Establishments with a limited choice of dishes may not have a printed menu but a selection of changing daily specials.

YOU MAY SEE…

MENIU FIX	set menu
LISTĂ DE VINURI	wine list
MÂNCĂRURI PENTRU VEGETARIENI	vegetarian dishes
SPECIALITĂȚI ALE ZILEI	specials of the day
PREȚ	price
SERVICIUL ESTE INCLUS	service included

YOU MAY HEAR...

Ce doriţi? *cheh doreetsy*	What would you like?
Ce doriţi să beţi? *cheh doreetsy ser betsy*	What would you like to drink?
Nu avem ... *noo avem...*	We don't have ...

Cooking Methods

baked	**copt** *copt*
boiled	**fiert** *fyert*
braised	**fiert înăbuşit** *fyert uhnerboosheet*
breaded	**pane** *paneh*
creamed	**piure** *pyooreoo*
diced	**tăiate în cubuleţe** *teryateh uhn coobooletseh*
filleted	**muşchi filet** *mooshky feeleh*
fried	**prăjit** *prerzheet*
grilled	**la grătar** *la grertar*
marinated	**marinat** *mareenat*
poached	**fiert în apă** *fyert uhn aper*
roasted	**prăjit** *prerzheet*
sautéed	**sotat** *sotat*
smoked	**afumat** *afoomat*
steamed	**în aburi** *uhn aboory*
stewed	**fiert înăbuşit** *fyert uhnerboosheet*
stuffed	**umplut** *oomploot*

Dietary Requirements

I'm diabetic	**Sunt diabetic m/diabetică f** soont dee-abeteec/ dee-abeteecer
I'm lactose intolerant	**Am intoleranță la lactoză** Am eentolerantser lah lactozer
I'm vegetarian	**Sunt vegetarian** soont vejetaree-an
I'm vegan	**Sunt vegan** soont vegan
I'm allergic to...	**Sunt alergic la...** soont alerjeec la...
I can't eat...	**Nu pot mânca...** noo pot muhnca...
dairy products	**produse lactate** prodooseh lactateh
gluten	**gluten** glyooten
nuts	**nuci** noocchy
pork	**carne de porc** carneh deh porc
shellfish	**crustacee** croostacheh-eh
spicy foods	**alimente picante** aleementeh peecanteh
wheat	**grâu** gruhᵒᵒ
Is it halal/kosher?	**Este halal/cușer?** Yesteh halal/coosher
Do you have...?	**Aveți ...?** Avetsy...
skimmed milk	**lapte degresat** lapteh degresat
whole milk	**lapte integral** lapteh eentegral
soya milk	**lapte de soia** lapteh deh soyah

Dining with Children

Do you have children's portions?	**Aveți porții pentru copii?** Avetsy portseey pentroo copeey
A highchair/child's seat, please.	**Un scaun pentru copil, vă rog.** Oon scaoon pentroo copeel, ver rog
Where can I feed/ change the baby?	**Unde aș putea hrăni/schimba copilul?** Oondeh ash pooteh-a hrernee/skeemba copeelool
Can you warm this?	**Puteți încălzi asta?** Pootetsy uhncerlzee astah

For Traveling with Children, see page 144.

How to Complain

When will our food be ready?	**Când va fi gata mâncarea noastră?** *Cuhnd va fee gata muhncareh-a nwastrer*
We can't wait any longer.	**Nu mai putem aştepta.** *Noo migh pootem ashtepta*
We're leaving.	**Plecăm.** *Plecerm*
I didn't order this.	**Nu am comandat aceasta.** *noo am comandat achasta*
I ordered...	**Am comandat ...** *am comandat*
I can't eat this.	**Nu pot mânca asta.** *noo pot muhnca asta*
This is too...	**Asta este prea...** *asta yesteh preh-a*
cold/hot	**rece/fierbinte** *recheh/fyerbeenteh*
salty/spicy	**sărată/picantă** *serrater/peecanter*
tough/bland	**tare/insipid** *tareh/eenseepeed*
This isn't clean/fresh.	**Asta nu este curat/proaspăt.** *asta noo yesteh coorat/prwaspert*

Paying

The check [bill], please.	**Nota de plată, vă rog.** *Notah deh plater, ver rog*
Separate checks [bills], please.	**Vrem să plătim separat.** *Vrem ser plerteem separat*
It's all together.	**Plătim împreună.** *Plerteem uhmpre-ooner*
Is service included?	**Serviciul este inclus?** *serveechyool yesteh eencloos*

It is customary to leave a tip if the service has been good. Most restaurants expect payment in cash but some large hotels will accept credit cards.

What's this amount for?	**Ce reprezintă suma aceasta?**
	cheh reprezeenter sooma achasta
I didn't have that.	**Nu am comandat asta.** *Noo am comandat asta*
I had...	**Am comandat...** *Am comandat...*
Can I have a receipt/ itemized bill?	**Puteți să-mi dați o chitanță/notă de plată detaliată?** *pootetsy sermy datsy o keetantser/noter deh plater detaliater*
That was delicious!	**Mâncarea a fost delicioasă!**
	muhncareh-a a fost deleechywaser
I've already paid	**Am plătit deja** *Am plerteet dezha.*

Meals & Cooking

Traditionally Romanians eat three meals a day:

Breakfast (micul dejun) is normally served between 7:00 and 10:00 a.m. and generally consists of some bread and cheese or jam, served with tea or coffee.

Lunch (masa de prânz or **dejunul)** is served from 12:00 noon until 2:00 p.m., and is considered the main meal of the day. A typical meal includes borsh or soup, followed by a stew or roast dinner. Homemade cakes such as pancakes, fritters or petits fours serve as dessert.

Dinner (cina) is taken between 7:00 and 10:00 p.m. It generally comprises of lighter dishes such as baked meat, pies, souffles, meat rolls, cheese rolls, **mămăligă** (polenta, or cornmeal porridge) with cheese and fried eggs, and home-made yoghurt.

Breakfast

I'd like breakfast, please.	**Aş dori micul dejun, vă rog.** *ash doree meecool dezhoon ver rog*
I'll have (a/an/some) ...	**Aş dori ...** *ash doree*
bacon	**slănină** *slerneener*
bacon and eggs	**slănină şi ouă** *slerneener shee o-wer*
bread	**pâine** *puhyneh*
butter	**unt** *oont*
cheese	**brânză** *bruhnzer*
coffee/tea...	**cafea/ceai** *cafeh-a/chay*
black	**neagră** *neh-agrer*
decaf	**decofeinizată** *dekofeh-eeneezater*
with	**cu** *coo*
artificial sweetener	**îndulcitor artificial** *undoolchitor arteefeecyal*
lemon	**lămâie** *lermuhyeh*
milk	**lapte** *lapteh*
sugar	**zahăr** *zaherr*
cold/hot cereal	**cereale calde/reci** *cherehaleh caldeh/rechy*
cold cuts	**mezeluri** *mezeloory*
eggs	**ouă** *o-wer*
fried eggs	**ouă prăjite/ochiuri** *o-wer prerzheeteh/okyoory*
ham and eggs	**şuncă şi ouă** *shooncer shee o-wer*
scrambled eggs	**ouă jumări** *o-wer zhoomery*
poached eggs	**ouă ochiuri fierte în apă** *o-wer okyoory fyerteh uhn aper*
omelet	**omletă** *omleter*
granola [muesli]	**baton de cereale (musli)** *baton deh chehreh-aleh (myooslee)*
honey	**miere** *myereh*
hot chocolate	**ciocolată fierbinte** *chocolater fyehrbeenteh*

jam/jelly	**gem/jeleu** *jem/jele*oo
. . .juice	**suc de...** *sooc deh*
apple	**mere** *mereh*
grapefruit	**grepfrut** *grepfroot*
orange	**portocale** *portocaleh*
marmalade	**marmeladă** *marmelader*
oatmeal	**fulgi de ovăz** *fooljy deh overz*
roll	**chifle** *keefleh*
toast	**pâine prăjită** *puhyneh prerzheeter*
sausage	**cârnați** *cuhrnatsy*
water	**apă** *aper*
yogurt	**iaurt** *yaoort*

The Romanian breakfast can be a very substantial meal consisting of bread or rolls with jam, cheese, salami, fried eggs, tomatoes and coffee or tea. Hotels serve either a continental breakfast of rolls, butter, jam, coffee or tea or a traditional breakfast with eggs, cold meats, cheese or yoghurt. Breakfast cereals are not common in Romania.

Appetizers

A typical Romanian starter is a platter of feta cheese, sliced salami and black olives. In summer you may also be served traditional aubergine salad (**salată de vinete**).

mititei/mici
meeteeteh^y/meech^y

a traditional dish of small, sausage-shaped minced meat rissoles (made with a mix of meats), served with garlic sauce.

cabanos prăjit *cabanos prerjeet* — fried pieces of sausage
cârnaţi cu usturoi *cuhrnats^y coo oostooro^y* — garlic sausage
caşcaval pané
cashcaval paneh — cheese coated in egg and breadcrumbs and deep fried.
chifteluţe *keeftelootseh* — fried minced meat balls
covrigei *covreegeh^y* — savoury pretzels
creier pané *creyer paneh* — brains in breadcrumbs
crenvurşti *crenvoorsht^y* — frankfurter
crochete de caşcaval
croketeh deh cashcaval — grated cheese mixed with egg and flour into croquettes and fried

drob de miel
drob deh myel — chopped lamb's liver and kidneys, mixed with herbs and egg and baked in the oven.

ficăţei de pasăre *feecertseh^y deh paserreh* — fried or braised chicken liver
frigărui *freegerroo^y* — grilled pork kebabs
măsline *mersleeneh* — olives

mezeluri *mezeloory*
mușchi filet *mooshky feeleh*
ouă umplute *o-wer oomplooteh*

pastramă *pastramer*
paté de ficat *pateh deh feecat*
piftie de pui
peefteeyeh deh pooy
pateuri cu carne
pateoory coo carneh
roșii *rosheey*
ruladă de cașcaval
roolader deh cashcaval
ruladă de ciuperci
roolader deh chooperchy
salată de boeuf
salater deh boef

assortment of cold meats
processed pork sirloin
hard-boiled eggs, halved,
then filled with paté and
topped with mayonnaise.
smoked mutton
liver paté
a traditional Romanian dish
of stewed chicken pieces in
puff pastry cases filled with
minced meat.
tomatoes
a sponge roll filled with
grated cheese and cream.
mushroom-filled sponge roll.

a salad of diced potatoes,
carrots, celery, pickled
cucumbers, peas and beef or
chicken meat in a
mayonnaise dressing.

salată de crudități
*salater deh croodeeterts*y
coarsely grated raw celery, carrots and apples in mayonnaise.

salată de icre *salater deh eecreh*
fish roe salad (taramasalata)

salată orientală
salater oryentaler
sliced potatoes, hard-boiled eggs, onions and olives marinated in a vinegar sauce.

salată de vinete *salater deh veeneteh*
aubergine salad

sardele *sardeleh*
sardines

şuncă *shooncer*
ham

Soup & Stews

borş cu carne de porc
borsh coo carneh deh porc
pork boiled with vegetables, and seasoned with tarragon, then soured.

borş de legume *borsh deh legoomeh*
vegetable borsh

borş de perişoare
borsh deh pereeshwareh
soured, seasoned vegetable soup served with rice-and-meat balls.

borş de văcuță
borsh deh vercootser
beef on the bone boiled with vegetables, seasoned with herbs and soured.

borş de vițel
borsh deh veetsel
veal boiled with vegetables and seasoned with herbs, then soured.

ciorbă de legume *chorber deh legoomeh*
vegetable ciorbă

ghiveci de legume
geevechy deh legoomeh
vegetable stew, with or without meat

supă de cartofi *sooper deh cartofy*
potato soup with vegetables

supă de pasăre *sooper deh paserreh*
clear chicken soup

supă de roşii *sooper deh rosheey*
tomato soup

supă-cremă de ciuperci	cream of mushroom soup
sooper cremer deh chooperchy	
supă-cremă de legume	thick vegetable purée soup
sooper cremer deh legoomeh	
supă-cremă de ţelină	cream of celery soup
sooper cremer deh tseleener	
tocană *tocaner*	stew
tocană de legume *tocaner deh legoomeh*	vegetable stew
tocăniţă de cartofi cu carne	vegetable stew with meat,
tocerneetser deh cartofy coo carneh	usually pork

The most popular soup in Romania is **borş**. This is a richly
flavored meat and vegetable soup soured with 'borsh' or lemon
juice and dressed with sour cream. Soup which has been soured with
lemon juice or yoghurt is called **ciorbă**, and you will frequently see
this on restaurant menus instead of **borş**. Soups in the countryside are
generally eaten with **mămăligă** (polenta).
Vegetarians should specify **fără carne** (without meat) when ordering
soups or stews.

Fish & Seafood

biban *beeban*	river perch
caviar *cavyar*	caviar
cegă *cheger*	sterlet
chefal *kefal*	grey mullet
chifteluţe de icre	caviar or fish roe dipped in
keeftelootseh deh eecreh	egg and breadcrumbs and
	fried in oil.

crab *crab*
crab

crap *crap*
carp

creveți *cre<u>vets</u>^y*
shrimps

fructe de mare *<u>froocteh</u> deh <u>mareh</u>*
seafood

ghiveci de pește
gee<u>vech</u>^y deh <u>peshteh</u>
a typical fish stew with olives, carrots, celery, cucumber and tomato purée.

homar *<u>homar</u>*
lobster

icre *<u>eecreh</u>*
fish roe

icre negre *<u>eecreh</u> <u>negreh</u>*
caviar

macrou *<u>macro</u>^{oo}*
mackerel

marinată de pește *maree<u>nater</u> deh <u>peshteh</u>*
fish marinated in brine.

păstrăv afumat
<u>perstrerv</u> afoo<u>mat</u>
a traditional dish of trout wrapped in fir tree branches and smoked.

păstrăv cu orez
<u>perstrerv</u> coo orez
trout cooked with onion, paprika and curry powder and served with rice.

pește à la grecque
<u>peshteh</u> a la grec
fried fish served with lemon juice and parsley.

peşte cu usturoi *peshteh coo oostooroy*
fish served in a tangy garlic sauce.

peşte la cuptor *peshteh la cooptor*
a whole fish, generally carp or pike, baked in the oven with tomatoes, carrots and green peppers.

peşte pané *peshteh paneh*
fish coated in beaten egg and flour, then fried in oil and served with lemon juice.

plătică *plerteecer*
river bream

raci *rachy*
freshwater crayfish

sardele *sardeleh*
sardines

scrumbie *scroombee-eh*
shad

sturion *stooryon*
sturgeon

sturion la grătar *stooryon la grertar*
grilled sturgeon

ştiucă *shtyoocer*
pike

ţipar *tseepar*
eel

Meat & Poultry

bibilică *beebeeleecer*
guinea fowl

caltaboş cu sânge *caltabosh coo suhnjeh*
black pudding

cap de porc *cap deh porc*
pig's head

căprioară *cerpreewarer*
venison

cârnaţi *cuhrnatsy*
sausage

carne de porc *carneh deh porc*
pork

carne de vacă *carneh deh vacer*
beef

chiftele *keefteleh*
meatballs

ciulama de pui *choolama deh pooy*
a traditional Romanian dish consisting of pieces of chicken cooked in a white cream sauce and flavoured with herbs.

clapon *clapon*	capon
coadă de vacă *cwader deh vacer*	oxtail
cotlet *cotlet*	chop/cutlet
curcan *coorcan*	turkey
escalop *escalop*	escalope
fazan *fazan*	pheasant
fazan cu smântână şi ciuperci *fazan coo smuhntuhner shee chooperchy*	pheasant with cream and mushrooms
ficăţei de pasăre *feecertsay deh paserreh*	braised or fried chicken liver
filet chateaubriand *feeleh chateaubriand*	tenderloin
friptură de curcan *freeptoorer deh coorcan*	roast turkey
friptură de pui *freeptoorer deh pooy*	roast chicken
friptură la tavă *freeptoorer la taver*	pot roast
găină umplută *gereener oomplooter*	whole chicken stuffed with liver, egg, breadcrumbs and herbs
gâscă *guhscer*	goose
ghiveci de curcan *geevechy deh coorcan*	turkey with aubergines simmered in wine
iepure *yepooreh*	rabbit
iepure de câmp *yepooreh deh cuhmp*	hare
iepure în vin roşu *yepooreh uhn veen roshoo*	rabbit cooked in red wine
iepure înăbuşit *yepooreh uhnerboosheet*	jugged hare (stew)
lişiţă *leesheetser*	teal (duck)

limbă *leember* — tongue

mâncare de iepure cu măsline — rabbit with olives,
muhncareh deh yepooreh coo mersleeneh — served cold

măruntaie de porc — chitterlings/chitlins
merroontayeh deh porc — (pork intestines)

mușchi de vacă *mooshky deh vacer* — sirloin

mușchi filet *mooshky feeleh* — fillet

pateu de iepure *pateoo deh yepooreh* — rabbit pie

pateuri cu brânză — puff pastries filled with
pateoory coo bruhnzer — cheese

pateuri cu carne — puff pastries filled with meat
pateoory coo carneh

piept/pulpă/aripă — breast/leg/wing
pyept/poolper/areeper

pilaf de pui *peelaf deh pooy* — chicken with rice and herbs

porc mistreț *porc meestrets* — wild boar

porumbel sălbatic — pigeon
poroombel serlbateec

potârniche *potuhrneekeh* — grouse

potârniche *potuhrneekeh* — partridge

prepeliță *prepeleetser* — quail

pui *pooy* — chicken

pui cu ciuperci — chicken in a mushroom sauce
pooy coo chooperchy

pui cu mujdei — roasted chicken with a
pooy coo moozhdehy — garlic sauce

pui cu tarhon *pooy coo tarhon* — a popular Transylvanian dish
of chicken with tarragon,
sautéed with white wine,
root vegetables, green
peppers and sour cream

pui la ceaun *pooy la cheh-aoon*	chicken fried in oil
pui la grătar *pooy la grertar*	whole chicken roasted on a spit over an open fire
pui la rotişor *pooy la roteesor*	barbecued chicken
pulpă de miel *poolper de myehl*	leg of lamb
purcel de lapte *poorchel deh lapteh*	suckling pig
raţă *ratser*	duck
raţă pe varză *ratser peh varzer*	roast duck served with cabbage
raţă sălbatică cu varză acră *ratser serlbateecer coo varzer acrer*	wild duck with sauerkraut
raţă tânără *ratser tuhnerrer*	duckling
şuncă *shooncer*	ham
şuncă afumată *shooncer afoomater*	smoked ham
carne de viţel *carneh deh veetsel*	veal

Vegetables & Staples

andive *andeeveh*	endive
anghinare *angeenareh*	artichokes
verde/roşu *verdeh/roshoo*	green/red
ardei iute *ardehy yooteh*	chilli
bame *bameh*	okra
broccoli *brocolee*	broccoli
cartofi *cartofy*	potatoes
castane *castaneh*	chestnuts
castravete *castraveteh*	cucumber
ceapă *chaper*	onions
ciuperci *chooperchy*	mushrooms
conopidă *conopeeder*	cauliflower
dovleac *dovleh-ac*	vegetable marrow

dovlecei *dovlechey*   courgette [zucchini]

fasole (boabe) *fasoleh (bwabeh)*   beans

fasole neagră *fasoleh neh-agrer*   butter beans

fasole verde *fasoleh verdeh*   green beans

fasole mare *fasoleh mareh*   kidney beans

fasole de Lima *fasoleh deh leema*   lima beans

fasole fideluță *fasoleh feedelootser*   French beans

legume asortate *legoomeh asortateh*   mixed vegetables

linte *leenteh*   lentils

macaroane cu brânză   macaroni with cheese
macarwaneh coo bruhnzer

macaroane cu nuci   macaroni with nut sauce
macarwaneh coo noochy

mărar *merrar*   dill

morcovi *morcovy*   carrots

napi *napy*   turnips

porumb *poroomb*   sweetcorn

praz *praz*   leeks

ridichi *reedeeky*   radishes

roşii *rosheey*   tomatoes

salată de cartofi *salater deh cartofy*   potato salad

salată verde *salater verdeh*	lettuce
secărică *secerreecer*	fennel
sfeclă *sfecler*	beets
sfeclă roșie *sfecler roshee-eh*	beetroot
spanac *spanac*	spinach
sparanghel (vârfuri) *sparangel (vuhrfoory)*	asparagus (tips)
țelină *tseleener*	celery
varză *varzer*	cabbage
varză de Bruxelles *varzer deh brooxel*	Brussels sprouts
vinete *veeneteh*	aubergines [eggplant]
borș de cartofi *borsh deh cartofy*	potato borsh
cartofi prăjiți *cartofy prerzheetsy*	chips
găluști *gerlooshty*	semolina dumplings
găluști cu prune *gerlooshty coo prooneh*	balls of mashed potatoes with plums
mămăligă *mermerleeger*	polenta
musaca de cartofi *moosaca deh cartofy*	potato moussaka
salată orientală *salater oryentaler*	potato salad with onions, boiled eggs and black olives
balmuș *balmoosh*	butter and grated curd cheese wrapped in polenta, rolled into balls and served very hot with sour cream. They may be filled with ham, mushroom, cheese or boiled egg.
tocinei *tocheenay*	a Moldavian speciality of grated potato rissoles, bound with egg and fried in oil. Served with sour cream.

Fruit

afine _afeeneh_	blueberries
agrişe _agreesheh_	gooseberries
alune de pădure _alooneh deh perdooreh_	hazelnuts
ananas _ananas_	pineapple
arahide _araheedeh_	peanuts
banane _bananeh_	bananas
căpşune _cerpshooneh_	strawberries
castane _castaneh_	chestnuts
cireşe _cheeresheh_	cherries
coacăze negre _cwacerzeh negreh_	blackcurrants
curmale _coormaleh_	dates
fructe uscate _froocteh ooscateh_	dried fruit
grepfrut _grepfroot_	grapefruit
gutui _gootooy_	quinces
lămâi _lermuhy_	lemons
lămâie verde _lamuhyeh verdeh_	lime
mandarine _mandareeneh_	tangerine
mere _mereh_	apples
migdale _meegdaleh_	almonds
nucă de cocos _noocer deh cocos_	coconut

nuci *noochy*	walnuts
pere *pereh*	pears
pepene galben *pepeneh galben*	melon
piersici *pyerseechy*	peaches
portocale *portocaleh*	oranges
prune *prooneh*	plums
prune uscate *prooneh ooscateh*	prunes
smochine *smokeeneh*	figs
stafide *stafeedeh*	raisins
struguri *stroogoory*	grapes
zmeură *zmeh-oorer*	raspberries

Cheese

brânză afumată *bruhnzer afoomater*	smoked cheese
brânză topită *bruhnzer topeeter*	processed cheese
brânză de vaci *bruhnzer deh vachy*	cottage cheese
cașcaval *cashcaval*	a type of cheddar
șvaițer *shvaytser*	a type of Swiss cheese with holes
caș *cash*	an unsalted feta cheese made from ewe's milk.

telemea *telemeh-a* — caş that has been stored in salted brine.

urdă <u>oo</u>rder — a soft unfermented cheese made from ewe's milk.

Dessert

baclava *bacla<u>va</u>* — a flaky pastry pie from Turkey, filled with nuts and sweetened with syrup.

bezele *be<u>ze</u>leh* — small meringues

budincă de brânză de vaci *boo<u>deen</u>cer deh <u>bruhn</u>zer deh vach^y* — sweetened cheese souffle

chec *kec* — rectangular sponge cake

clătite *cler<u>tee</u>teh* — crepes

clătite cu brânză *cler<u>tee</u>teh coo <u>bruhn</u>zer* — crepes filled with sweetened cheese mixed with egg

cozonac *cozo<u>nac</u>* — a large sweet loaf made with yeast, eggs and milk flavoured with nuts, raisins, poppy seeds or Turkish delight. This dessert is traditionally eaten at Easter and Christmas.

cremşnit *<u>crem</u>shneet* — millefeuille (napoleon)

dulceaţa *dool<u>chat</u>ser* — preserved whole fruits

fursecuri *foor<u>se</u>coor^y* — small biscuits or tea cakes

gogoşi *go<u>gosh</u>^y* — doughnuts

înghetaţă *uhn<u>get</u>sater* — ice cream

lapte de pasăre *<u>lap</u>teh deh <u>pa</u>serreh* — `floating islands´: egg whites beaten with sugar until stiff and served floating on

a custard sauce.

napolitane *napoleetaneh* — wafers with filling

papanaşi *papanashy* — a traditional dessert made from cottage cheese, eggs and sugar, formed into flattened rounds and fried or boiled. Usually served with cream or jam.

pandişpan *pandeeshpan* — sponge cake

pască *pascer* — an Easter treat consisting of yeast dough cases filled with chocolate or soft cheese and raisins

plăcintă *plercheenter* — flaky pastry pie

prăjitură *prerzheetoorer* — an individual torte

salată de fructe *salater deh froocteh* — fruit salad

savarină *savareener* — a round sponge cake moistened in syrup and filled with whipped cream.

spumă de fragi *spoomer deh frajy* — wild strawberry mousse

ştrudel cu mere *shtroodel coo mereh* — apple strudel

tartă cu fructe _tarter coo froocteh_	small round fruit tart
tort _tort_	large layer cake
tort de bezea _tort deh bezeh-a_	layered cream meringue
tort de nuci _tort deh noochy_	walnut layer cake
tort Joffre _tort zhofr_	rich chocolate cake

Sauces & Condiments

ketchup _ketchoop_	ketchup
mujdei de usturoi _moozhdey deh oostooroy_	garlic sauce
muştar _mooshtar_	mustard
oţet _otset_	vinegar
piper _peeper_	pepper
sare _sareh_	salt
ulei _oolehy_	oil

At the Market

Where are the trolleys/baskets?	**Unde sunt cărucioarele/coşurile?** _oondeh soont cer-rootchwareleh/coshooreeleh_
Where is…?	**Unde este…?** _oondeh yesteh_
I'd like some of that/this.	**Nişte de asta/acela.** _neeshteh de asta/achela_
Can I taste it?	**Pot să gust?** _pot ser goost_
I'd like…	**Aş vrea …** _ash vreh-a_

YOU MAY HEAR…

Cu ce vă pot ajuta? _coo cheh ver pot azhoota_	Can I help you?
Ce doriţi? _cheh doreetsy_	What would you like?
Mai doriţi ceva? _migh doreetsy cheva_	Anything else?
Costă … lei. _coster… lehy_	That's…Lei.

a kilo/half kilo of…	**un kilogram/o jumătate de kilogram**
	oon keelogram/o zhoomertateh deh keelogram
a liter of…	**un litru de…** *oon leetroo deh…*
a piece of…	**o bucată de …** *o boocater deh…*
a slice of…	**o felie de…** *o felee-eh deh…*
More./Less.	**Mai mult/Mai puțin** *migh moolt/migh pootseen*
How much?	**Cât costă?** *cuht coster*

Measurements in Europe are metric, and that applies to the weight of food too. If you tend to think in pounds and ounces, it's worth brushing up on what the metric equivalent is before you go shopping for fruit and veg in markets and supermarkets. Five hundred grams, or half a kilo, is a common quantity to order, and that converts to just over a pound (17.65 ounces, to be precise).

YOU MAY SEE…

A se utiliza înainte de …	use by…
a seh ooteeleeza uhnaeenteh deh…	
calorii *caloreey*	calories
fără grăsimi *fer-rer grerseemy*	fat free
A se păstra la rece *a seh perstra la reche*	keep refrigerated
Poate să conțină urme de…	may contain traces of…
pwateh ser contseener oormeh deh…	
Pentru cuptorul cu microunde	microwaveable
pentroo cooptorool coo meecro-oondeh	
Comercializat de… *comerchee-aleezat deh…*	sell by…
Recomandat pentru vegetarieni	suitable for vegetarians
recomandat pentroo vejetaryeny	

Where do I pay?	**Unde plătesc?** _oondeh_ _plertesc_
A bag, please.	**O pungă, vă rog.** _oh_ _poonger,ver rog_
I'm being helped.	**Sunt ajutat.** _soont azhootat_

For Conversion Tables, see page 170.

In the Kitchen

deschizător de sticle _deskeezertor deh steecleh_	bottle opener
castron _castron_	bowl
deschizător de conserve _deskeezertor deh conserveh_	can opener
tirbuşon _teerbooshon_	corkscrew
o ceaşcă _o chashcer_	a cup
o furculiţă _o foorcooleetser_	a fork
tigaie _teega-yeh_	frying pan
un pahar _oon pahar_	a glass
un cuţit _oon cutseet_	a (steak) knife
cană gradată/lingură de măsurare _caner gradater/leengoorer deh mersoorareh_	measuring cup/spoon
un şerveţel _oon shervetsel_	a napkin
o farfurie _o farfooree-eh_	a plate

oală _waler_	pot
spatulă _spatooler_	spatula
o lingură _o leengoorer_	a spoon

For Meals & Cooking, see page 65.

Drinks

ESSENTIAL

The wine list/drink menu, please.	**Puteţi să-mi daţi lista de vinuri, vă rog?** _pootetsy sermy datsy leesta deh veenoory ver rog_
What do you recommend?	**Ce îmi recomandaţi?** _cheh uhmy recomandatsy_
I'd like a bottle/glass of red/white wine.	**Aş vrea o sticlă/un pahar de vin roşu/alb.** _ash vreh-a o steecler deh veen roshoo/alb_
The house wine, please.	**Vinul casei, vă rog.** _Veenool casey, ver rog_
Another bottle/glass, please.	**Mai aduceţi-mi o sticlă/un pahar de …, vă rog.** _migh adoochetseemy o steecler/oon pahar deh … ver rog_
I'd like a local beer.	**Aş vrea o bere locală.** _ash vreh-a o bereh localer_
What would you like to drink?	**Ce doriţi să beţi?** _cheh doreetsy ser betsy_
Cheers!	**Noroc!** _noroc_
A coffee/tea, please.	**O cafea/un ceai, vă rog.** _o cafeh-a/oon chay ver rog_
Black.	**neagră** _neh-agrer_
With…	**cu** _coo_
milk	**lapte** _lapteh_
sugar	**zahăr** _zaherr_
artificial sweetener	**îndulcitor artificial** _undoolchitor arteefeecyal_

A..., please.	..., vă rog. _oon_..., _ver rog._
juice	**un suc** _oon sooc_
soda	**un sifon** _oon seefon_
sparkling/still water	**O apă gazoasă/plată** _oh aper gazwaser/plater_

Non-alcoholic Drinks

cafea _cafeh-a_	coffee
ciocolată fierbinte _chocolater fyehrbeenteh_	hot chocolate
limonadă _leemonader_	lemonade
apă gazoasă/plată _aper gazwaser/plater_	sparkling/still water
suc _sooc_	juice
lapte _lapteh_	milk
sifon _seefon_	soda
ceai cu gheaţă _chay coo gyatser_	iced tea
ceai _chay_	tea
suc de roşii _sooc deh rosheey_	tomato juice
apă tonică _aper toneecer_	tonic water
cafea turcească _cafeh-a toorchashcer_	Turkish coffee

Cafe-bar serve hot beverages, soft and alcoholic drinks, and are a convenient place for a quick snack. Cafe-bars are similar to snack bars, which also offer a range of light meals and drinks. Cofetărie are cake shops that also serve coffee, ice cream and soft drinks. Tea is generally served only in large hotels and Turkish coffee is usually served at the end of the meal in a restaurant. It is safe to drink tap water.

YOU MAY HEAR...

Ce doriți să beți? *cheh doreetsy ser betsy*	Can I get you a drink?
Cu lapte sau zahăr? *coo lapteh saoo zaher*	With milk or sugar?
Apă gazoasă sau plată? *aper gazwaser saoo plater*	Sparkling or still water?

Aperitifs, Cocktails & Liqueurs

țuică *tzooyker*	brandy
gin *jeen*	gin
lichior *leekyor*	liquer
rom *rom*	rum
whisky scoțian *weeskee scotsee-an*	scotch
tequila *tekila*	tequila
vodcă *vodcer*	vodka
whisky *weesky*	whisky

Beer

bere *bereh*	beer
la sticlă/la halbă *la steecler/la halber*	bottled/draft

For a traditional, male, drinking experience, **Berărie** are public houses where you can drink Romanian beer as well as foreign brands. Please note, women do not usually frequent these places and are better off trying a **braserie**, a combined bar, cafe and restaurant. **Podgorie** are wine bars that serve drinks only.

National drinks include **ţuică**, a plum brandy, **vişinată**, a liquor made from cherry syrup and white spirit, and vodka. Another option is **bragă**, a sweet and refreshing, low alcohol, bread beer, sold by itinerant street-sellers from barrels.

neagră/cu conţinut redus de alcool	dark/light
neh-agrer/coo contseenoot redoos deh alco-ol	
lager/pilsen *lager/peelsen*	lager/pilsener
local/importat *local/eemportat*	local/imported
fără alcool *farer alcohohl*	non-alcoholic

Wine

vin *veen*	wine
roşu/alb *roshoo/alb*	red/white

Apart from national brands of beer, commonly sold in 1/2-litre bottles, many types of foreign beer are available in cans, but you'll find the national brands cheaper and worth a try. Look out for **Silva**, **Ursus**, **Gambrinus** or **Timişoreana** which are the most popular brands. The standard national measure is the **halbă**, roughly equivalent to half a litre. The name derives from the German 'half litre' and describes the large glass mug in which beer is generally served.

al casei/de masă *al casehv/deh maser*	house/table
sec/dulce *sec/doolcheh*	dry/sweet
spumos *spoomos*	sparkling
şampanie *shampanyeh*	champagne
vin pentru desert *veen pentroo desert*	dessert wine

Romania produces many wines of worldwide renown. From the North of Moldova comes the famous wine of **Cotnari**. Further south there are other well-known vineyards such as **Panciu**, **Nicoreşti**, **Coteşti**, **Jariştea** and **Odobeşti**. They produce varieties such as **Pinot Gris**, **Riesling** and **Fetească**. In Wallachia the vine cultures of **Dealu Mare**, **Valea Călugărească**, **Urlaţi**, **Tohani** and **Pietroasele** are equally famed, with two varieties particularly appreciated: **Tămâioasa** of **Pietroasele** and the **Busuioaca** of **Valea Călugărească**. Sweet wines come from the vineyards of **Murfatlar** and **Babadag**, and in Transylvania the wines from the **Târnave** vineyards are also widely enjoyed. Larger, well-stocked supermarkets and good restaurants also have a large selection of imported wines. **Un şprit** (wine spritzer) is popular at mealtimes.

afină *afeener*		blueberry
alune de pădure *alooneh deh perdooreh*		hazelnut
ananas *ananas*		pineapple
andive *andeeveh*		endive [chicory]
anghinare *angeenareh*		artichoke
antreuri *antreoory*		appetizers
apă *aper*		water
apă tonică *aper toneecer*		tonic water
arahidă *araheeder*		peanut
ardei gras *ardehy gras*		sweet pepper
arpagic *arpageec*		chives
bame *bameh*		okra
banană *bananeh*		banana
băuturi răcoritoare *baᵒᵒtoory rercoreetwareh*		soft drinks
bere *bereh*		beer
brânză *bruhnzer*		cheese
brânză albastră *bruhnzer albastrer*		blue cheese
busuioc *busooyoc*		basil
cafea *cafeh-a*		coffee
caise *caeeseh*		apricot
căpșună *cerpshooner*		strawberry
capere *capehreh*		caper
căprioară *cerpreewarer*		venison
cârnați *cuhrnatsy*		sausage
carne de miel *car-neh deh myel*		lamb
carne *carneh*		meat

cârnaț *cuhrnats*	sausage
cartofi *cartofy*	potato
cartofi dulci *cartofy doolchy*	sweet potato
cartofi prăjiți *cartofy prerzheetsy*	French fries
castană *castaner*	chestnut
castravete *castraveteh*	cucumber
castravecior *castravehchyor*	gherkin/pickle
carne de pasăre *carneh deh paserreh*	poultry
ceai *chay*	tea
ceapă de apă *chaper deh aper*	shallot
ceapă *chaper*	onion
ceapă verde *chaper verdeh*	scallion [spring onion]
cereală *cherealer*	cereal
chiflă *cheefler*	roll
chiftele *keefteleh*	burgers
chipsuri de cartofi *cheepsury deh cartofy*	potato chips [crisps]
cimbru *cheembroo*	thyme
ciocolată *chocolater*	chocolate
cireşe *cheeresheh*	cherries
ciupercă *cyoopercer*	mushroom
coacăze negre *cwacerzeh negreh*	blackcurrants
coadă de vacă *cwader deh vacer*	oxtail
cod *cod*	cod
conopidă *conopeeder*	cauliflower
coriandru *coreeandru*	cilantro [coriander]
cotlet *cotlet*	chop
covrigi *covreejy*	pretzels

crenvurşti *crenvoorshty* — hot dog sausage
crevete *cruhveht* — shrimp/prawn
croissant *crwahsawnt* — croissant
cuburi de gheaţă *cuburee deh gheater* — ice (cubes)
cuişoare *cuishwareh* — clove
curcan *curcan* — turkey
deserturi *desertoory* — desserts
dovlecei *dovlecey* — zucchini [courgette]
dropsuri *dropsoory* — candy [sweets]
dulciuri *doolchoory* — sweets
fasole *fasoleh* — beans
fasole verde *fasoleh verdeh* — green beans
fazan *fazan* — pheasant
ficat *feecat* — liver
foi de dafin *foi deh dafeen* — bay leaf
friptură *freeptoorer* — roast
friptură de vacă *freeptoorer deh vacer* — roast beef
frişcă *freshcer* — cream
fructe *froocteh* — fruit
fructe de mare *froocteh deh mareh* — seafood

fursec *foorsec*	cookie [biscuit]
fursecuri *foorsecoory*	cookies
gâscă *guhscer*	goose
gem *jem*	jam
ghimber *gheember*	ginger
gin *jeen*	gin
grepfrut *grepfroot*	grapefruit
gustări *goosterry*	snacks
hamburgher *hamburgehr*	hamburger
homar *homar*	lobster
iaurt *yaoort*	yoghurt
iepure *yepooreh*	rabbit
înghețată *uhngetsater*	ice cream
lămâie *lermuhyeh*	lemon
lămâie verde *lamuhyeh verdeh*	lime
lapte *lapteh*	milk
lapte de soia *lapte deh soya*	soya milk
legume *legoomeh*	vegetables
limbă *leember*	tongue
linte *leenteh*	lentils

macaroane *macarwaneh*		macaroni
măcriş *mercreesh*		watercress
macrou *macro͞o*		mackerel
maioneză *mighonezer*		mayonnaise
mâncăruri cu ouă		egg dishes
muhncerroory coo o-wer		
mandarină *mandareener*		tangerine
măr *mer*		apple
mărar *merrar*		dill
marmeladă *marmelader*		marmalade
măslină *mersliner*		olive
mazăre *mazerreh*		peas
mentă *menter*		mint
mezeluri *mezeloory*		cold cuts
miere *myereh*		honey
migdale *meegdaleh*		almonds
mirodenii *meerodeneey*		herbs
morcov *morcov*		carrot
mură *moorer*		blackberry
nap *nap*		turnip
nucşoară *noocshwarer*		nutmeg
nucă de cocos *noocer deh cocos*		coconut
nuci *noocchy*		nuts
oaie *waye*		mutton
omletă *omleter*		omelet
oregano *oregano*		oregano
orez *orez*		rice
ou *oho͞o*		egg
pâine *puhyneh*		bread
pâine prăjită *puhyneh prerzheeter*		toast

pară *parer*		pear
păsări *persery*		poultry
paste făinoase *pasteh fer-eenwaseh*		pasta
păstrăv *perstrerv*		trout
patiserie *pateeseree-eh*		pastries
pătrunjel *pertroongel*		parsley
pere *pereh*		pears
peşte *peshteh*		fish
pepene galben *pepeneh galben*		melon
pepene roşu *pepeneh roshoo*		watermelon
picior *peecyor*		leg
piept de găină *pyept deh gereener*		breast (of chicken)
piersică *pierseecer*		peach
piper *peeperr*		pepper (vegetable)
pizza *peetsah*		pizza
porc *porc*		pork
port *port*		port
portocală *portocaler*		orange
porumb *poroomb*		sweet corn
prăjitură *prerzheetoorer*		tart
praz *praz*		leek
prepeliţă *prepeleetser*		quail
prună *prooner*		plum
prune uscate *prooneh ooscateh*		prune
pui *pooy*		chicken
rac *rak*		crayfish (river)
raţă *ratser*		duck
ridiche *reedeeche*		radish
rinichi *reeneeky*		kidney
roşie *roshee-ehy*		tomato
rozmarin *rozmarin*		rosemary

rubarbă *rubarber*	rhubarb
salam *salam*	salami
salată *salater*	salad
salată verde *salateh verdeh*	lettuce
salate *salateh*	salads
săndvici *sendveechy*	sandwich
supe *soopeh*	soups
salvie *salvye*	sage
sardele *sardeleh*	sardine
scorţişoară *scortsheeshwarer*	cinnamon
secărică *secerreecer*	fennel
sfeclă roşie *sfecler roshee-eh*	beetroot
slănină *slerneener*	bacon
smântână *smuhntuhner*	sour cream
smochină *smocheener*	fig
şofran *shofran*	saffron
somon *somon*	salmon
sos *sos*	sauce
spaghete *spagheteh*	spaghetti
spanac *spanac*	spinach

sparanghel *sparangel*	asparagus
stafidă *stafeeder*	raisin
struguri *stroogoory*	grapes
suc *sooc*	juice
şuncă *shooncer*	ham
supă *sooper*	soup
tăiţei *tereetsay*	noodle
tarhon *tarhon*	tarragon
ţelină *tsehleener*	celery
ţipar *tseepar*	eel
tocană *tocaner*	stew
tofu *tofoo*	tofu
ton *ton*	tuna
trufe *troofe*	truffle
unt *oont*	butter
usturoi *oostooroy*	garlic
vacă *vacer*	beef
vânat *vuhnat*	game
vânătă *vernerter*	eggplant [aubergine]
vanilie *vaneelee-eh*	vanilla

varză *varzer*   cabbage
varză de Bruxelles   Brussels sprouts
varzer deh Bruxelles

vin *veen*   wine
vițel *veetsel*   veal
zahăr *zaherr*   sugar
zmeură *zmeoorer*   raspberry

People

Conversation

ESSENTIAL

Hello!/Hi!	**Bună!**	_booner_
How are you?	**Ce mai faceţi?**	_cheh migh fachetsy_
Fine, thanks.	**Mulţumesc bine.**	_mooltsoomesc beeneh_
Excuse me!	**Pardon, vă rog!**	_pardon ver rog_
Do you speak English?	**Vorbiţi englezeşte?**	_Vorbeetsy englezeshteh_
What's your name?	**Cum vă numiţi?**	_coom ver noomeetsy_
My name is...	**Mă numesc...**	_mer noomesc..._
Nice to meet you.	**Încântat de cunoştinţă.**	_uhncuhntat deh coonoshteentser_
Where are you from?	**De unde veniţi?**	_deh oondeh veneetsy_
I'm from the	**Vin din**	_veen deen_
U.K./U.S.	**Marea Britanie/Statele Unite**	_Mareh-ah Breetanyeh/Stateleh Ooneeteh_
What do you do for a living?	**Cu ce vă ocupaţi?**	_coo cheh ver ocoopatsy_
I work for...	**Lucrez pentru...**	_Loocrez pentroo_
I'm a student.	**Sunt student.**	_soont stoodent_
I'm retired.	**Sunt pensionar.**	_Soont pensee-onar_
Do you like...?	**Doriţi...?**	_doreetsy_
Goodbye.	**La revedere.**	_la revedereh_
See you later.	**Pe curând.**	_peh cooruhnd_

Language Difficulties

Do you speak English?	**Vorbiţi englezeşte?**	_vorbeetsy englezeshteh_
Does anyone here speak English?	**Vorbeşte cineva aici englezeşte?**	_vorbeshteh cheeneva a-eechy englezeshteh_

I don't speak Romanian.	**Nu vorbesc româneşte.**
	noo vorbesc romuhnehshteh
Can you speak more slowly?	**Puteţi să vorbiţi mai rar, vă rog?**
	pootetsy ser vorbeetsy migh rar ver rog
Can you repeat that?	**Puteţi să repetaţi asta?** *pootetsy ser repetatsy asta*
Excuse me?	**Pardon, vă rog?** *pardon ver rog*
Can you spell it?	**Cum se scrie?** *coom seh scree-eh*
Please write it down.	**Vă rog scrieţi asta.** *ver rog scree-etsy asta*
Can you translate this into English for me?	**Puteţi să-mi traduceţi, vă rog, asta?**
	pootetsy sermy tradoo-chetsy ver rog asta
What does this/ that mean?	**Ce înseamnă asta?** *cheh uhnseh-amner asta*
I understand.	**Înţeleg.** *uhntseleg*
I don't understand.	**Nu înţeleg.** *noo uhntseleg*
Do you understand?	**Înţelegeţi?** *uhntselejetsy*

YOU MAY HEAR...

Vorbesc doar puţin engleza.	I only speak a little
Vorbesc dwar pootseen engleza.	English.
Nu vorbesc engleza. *Noo vorbesc engleza.*	I don't speak English.

Some older Romanians kiss a woman's hand when meeting them but foreign men are not expected to do this. Friends may kiss and hug when they meet – usually twice, once on each cheek. When addressing people, use **Domnul** for Mr. and **Doamna** for Mrs., followed by the person's surname. Good acquaintances may address each other using this title with the first name, but only close friends and family members use the first name on its own.

Making Friends

Hello!	**Bună!** _booner_
Good afternoon.	**Bună ziua.** _booner zeewah_
Good evening.	**Bună seara.** _booner seh-ara_
My name is...	**Mă numesc...** _mer noomesc_
What's your name?	**Cum vă numiți?** _coom ver noomeets__y_
I'd like to introduce you to...	**Dați-mi voie să vă prezint pe...** _datseem__y__ voyeh ser ver prezeent peh_
Pleased to meet you.	**Încântat de cunoștință.** _uhncuhntat deh coonoshteentser_
How are you?	**Ce mai faceți?** _cheh migh fachets__y_
Fine, thanks, and you?	**Bine, mulțumesc, și dumneavoastră?** _beeneh mooltsoomesc, shee doomnavwastrer_

Romanians have a reputation for being outgoing and friendly, and you should have no problem making friends. However, it is regarded as impolite if you address someone you don't know very well using the informal **tu.** This privilege is reserved for relatives, close friends and young people of a similar age and professional standing. Use the formal **dumneavoastră** until your acquaintance makes it clear that he or she wants you to use the more familiar form of address.

Travel Talk

I'm here...	**Sunt aici...** _soont a-eech__y_	
on business	**în interes de serviciu** _uhn eenteres deh serveechee-oo_	
on vacation [holiday]	**în vacanță** _uhn vacantser_	
studying	**pentru studii** _pentroo stoodee__y_	

I'm staying for...	**O să stau...** *o ser sta^{oo}*
I've been here...	**Sunt aici de...** <u>soo</u>nt *aechy deh...*
a day	**o zi** *o zee*
a week	**o săptămână** *o serptermuhner*
a month	**o lună** *o looner*
Where are you from?	**De unde veniţi?** *deh oondeh ven<u>eet</u>sy*
I'm from...	**Vin din...** *veen deen*

For Business Travel, see page 141.

Personal

Who are you with?	**Cu cine aţi venit?**
	Coo cheeneh atsy veneet
I'm here alone.	**Am venit singur.**
	Am veneet seengoor
I'm with...	**Sunt cu...** <u>soo</u>nt *coo*
my husband/wife	**soţul meu/soţia mea**
	sotsool me^{oo}/sotseea meh-a
my boyfriend/	**prietenul meu/prietena mea**
girlfriend	*pree-etenool me^{oo}/pree-etena meh-a*
a friend	**un prieten** *oon pree-ehten*
friends	**prietenii mei** *pree-ehteneey mey*
a colleague	**un coleg** *oon coleg*
colleagues	**colegii mei** *colejeey mey*
When's your birthday?	**Când este ziua dumneavoastră de naştere?**
	Cuhnd yesteh zeewah doomneh-avwastrer deh nashtereh
How old are you?	**Ce vârstă aveţi?/Câti ani ai?**
	cheh vuhrster a<u>vet</u>sy/cuhtsy any igh
I'm...	**Sunt...** *soont*
Are you married?	**Sunteţi căsătorit?**
	soontetsy cersertoreet

I'm...	**Sunt...** *soont*
single/in a	**necăsătorit/într-o relaţie**
relationship	*necersertoreet/uhntroh relatsee-eh*
engaged	**logodit** *logodeet*
married	**căsătorit** *cersertoreet*
divorced	**divorţat** *deevortsat*
separated	**despărţit** *despertseet*
widowed	**văduv** *verdoov*
Do you have children/ grandchildren?	**Aveţi copii/nepoţi?** *Avetsy copeey/nepotsy*

For Numbers, see page 166.

Work & School

What do you do for a living?	**Cu ce vă ocupaţi?** *coo cheh ver ocoopatsy*
What are you studying?	**Ce studiati?** *cheh stoodee-atsy*
I'm studying French.	**Studiez franceza.** *Stoodee-ehz francheza*
I...	**Eu...** *Yeoo*
work full-/ part-time	**lucrez cu normă întreagă/cu jumătate de normă** *loocrez coo normer uhntreh-ager/coo joomertateh deh normer*
am unemployed	**sunt şomer** *soont shomehr*
work at home	**lucrez la domiciliu** *loocrez la domeecheelyoo*
Who do you work for?	**Pentru cine lucraţi?** *Pentroo cheene loocratsy*
I work for...	**Lucrez pentru...** *Loocrez pentroo...*
Here's my business card.	**Aceasta este cartea mea de vizită.** *Achasta yesteh carteh-a meh-a deh veezeeter*

For Business Travel, see page 141.

Weather

What's the forecast?	**Ce vreme se prevede?**
	cheh vremeh she prevedeh
What beautiful/	**Ce vreme frumoasă/urâtă!**
terrible weather!	*Cheh vremeh froomwaser/ooruhter*
It's...	**Este...** *yesteh*
cool/warm	**rece/cald** *reche/cald*
cold/hot	**frig/foarte cald**
	freeg/fwarteh cald
rainy/sunny	**o zi ploioasă/senină**
	o zee ploywaser/seneener
snowy/icy	**o zi cu zăpadă/geroasă**
	oh zee coo zerpader/jerowaser
Do I need a jacket/	**Am nevoie de o jachetă/o umbrelă?**
an umbrella?	*Am nevoyeh deh oh jaketer/oombreler*

For Temperature, see page 171.

Romance

ESSENTIAL

Would you like to go out for a drink/dinner?	**Vrei să ieşim să bem ceva/să luăm cina?** *vrey ser yes<u>heem</u> ser <u>bem</u> cheva/ser <u>lwerm</u> cheenah*
What are your plans for tonight/tomorrow?	**Ce planuri ai pentru disearā/mâine?** *cheh plan<u>oor</u>y igh <u>pentroo</u> dee<u>seh</u>-arer/<u>muhy</u>neh*
Can I have your (phone) number?	**Îmi dai numărul tău de telefon?** *Uhmy <u>digh</u> <u>noo</u>mer-rool ter^{oo} deh <u>telefon</u>*
Can I join you?	**Pot să te însoţesc?** *pot ser teh uhnsot<u>esc</u>*
Can I buy you a drink?	**Ce doriţi să beţi?** *<u>cheh</u> dor<u>eets</u>y ser bets^y*
I love you.	**Te iubesc.** *teh yoo<u>besc</u>*

The Dating Game

Would you like to go out...?	**Pot să vă invit** *pot ser ver eenveet*
for coffee	**la cafea** *lah ca<u>feh-a</u>*
for a drink	**la o băutură** *la o berootoorer*
to dinner	**cina** *cheena*
What are your plans for...?	**Ce planuri ai pentru...?** *<u>Cheh</u> plan<u>oor</u>y igh pentroo...*
today	**azi** *az^y*
tonight	**deseară** *deseh-arer*
tomorrow	**mâine** *muhyⁿeh*
this weekend	**sfârşit de săptămână** *sfuhrsheet deh serptermuhner*
Where would you like to go?	**Unde ai vrea să mergi?** *Oondeh igh vreh-a ser merj^y*

I'd like to go to...	**Aş vrea să merg să...**
	ash vreh-a ser merg ser
Do you like...?	**Doriţi...?** *doreetsy*
Can I have your phone number/email?	**Îmi dai numărul tău de telefon/adresa ta de e-mail?** *Uhmy digh noomerool teroo deh telefon/ adresa ta deh ee-mayl*
Are you on Facebook/Twitter?	**Ai cont pe Facebook/Twitter?** *Igh cont peh Facebook/Twitter*
Can I join you?	**Pot să te însoţesc?** *Pot ser teh uhnsotsesc*
You're very attractive.	**Eşti foarte atrăgător m/atrăgătoare f.** *Yeshty fwarteh atrergertor/atrergertwareh*
Let's go somewhere quieter.	**Să mergem într-un loc mai liniştit.** *Ser merjem uhntroon loc migh leeneeshteet*

For Communications, see page 48.

Accepting & Rejecting

I'd love to.	**Cu plăcere.** *coo plerchereh*
Where should we meet?	**Unde ne întâlnim?** *oondeh neh uhntuhlneem*
I'll meet you at the bar/your hotel.	**Ne întâlnim la bar/la hotelul tău.** *Neh uhntuhlneem la bar/la hotelool teroo*
I'll come by at...	**O să vin la...** *Oh ser veen la...*
I'm busy.	**Sunt ocupat.** *soont ocoopat*
I'm not interested.	**Nu mă interesează.** *noo mer eenteresazer*
Leave me alone.	**Lăsaţi-mă în pace.** *lersasee-mer uhn pacheh*
Stop bothering me!	**Nu mă mai deranja!** *Noo mer migh deranzhah*

For Time, see page 168.

Getting Intimate

Can I hug/kiss you?	**Pot să te îmbrăţişez/să te sărut?**	
	Pot ser teh uhmbrertsee<u>shez</u>/ser teh ser-<u>root</u>	
Yes.	**Da.** *da*	
No.	**Nu.** *noo*	
Stop!	**Opreşte!** *opreshteh*	
I love you.	**Te iubesc.** *teh yoo<u>bes</u>c*	

Sexual Preferences

Are you gay?	**Eşti homosexual?**	
	Yesht^y homosexoo-al	
I'm...	**Sunt...** *<u>soo</u>nt*	
heterosexual	**heterosexual** *heterosex<u>oo</u>-al*	
homosexual	**homosexual** *homosex<u>oo</u>-al*	
bisexual	**bisexual** *beesex<u>oo</u>-al*	
Do you like men/	**Îţi plac bărbaţii/femeile?**	
women?	*Uhts^y plac ber-rbatsee^y/fe<u>meh</u>-eeleh*	

Leisure Time

ESSENTIAL

Where's the tourist information office?	**Unde se află oficiul de turism?**
	oondeh seh afler ofee-chee-ool deh tooreesm
What are the main sights?	**Care sunt obiectivele turistice importante?**
	careh soont obyectee-veleh tooreesteecheh eemportanteh
Do you offer tours in English?	**Oferiţi excursii în limba engleză?**
	Ofereetsy excoorseey uhn leembah englezer
Can I have a map/ guide?	**Îmi puteţi da o hartă/un ghid?**
	Uhmy pootetsy dah oh harter/oon geed

Tourist Information

Do you have information on…?	**Aveţi informaţii despre…?**
	Avetsy eenformatseey despreh…
Can you recommend…?	**Ne puteţi recomanda…?**
	neh pootetsy recomanda
a bus tour	**o excursie cu autocarul**
	o excoorsee-eh coo aootocarool
an excursion to…	**împrejurimi/o excursie?**
	uhmprezhooreemy/o ehxcoorsee-eh
a tour of…	**un traseu prin** _oon traseoo preen_

Tourist information offices are few and far between in Romania so it is best to do any research in advance. Visit www.romaniatourism.com for lists of attractions, itinerary ideas and general information.

On Tour

I'd like to go on the excursion to...	**Aş dori să vizitez...**	*Ash doree ser veezeetez...*
When's the next tour?	**Când este următoarea excursie?**	
	Cuhnd yesteh oormertwareh-a ehxcoorsee-eh	
Are there tours in English?	**Aveţi un ghid care vorbeşte englezeşte?**	
	avetsʸ oon geed careh vorbeshteh englezeshteh	
Is there an English guide book/ audio guide?	**Aveţi un ghid în engleza?**	
	avetsʸ oon geed uhn englezah	
What time do we leave/return?	**La ce oră plecăm/ne întoarcem?**	
	La cheh orer plecerm/neh uhntwarchem?	
We'd like to see...	**Am dori să vizităm...**	
	Am doree ser veezeeterm...	
Can we stop here...?	**Putem să ne oprim aici...?**	
	Pootem ser neh opreem a-eechʸ	
to take photos	**pentru a face fotografii**	
	pentroo a facheh fotografeeʸ	
for souvenirs	**pentru suveniruri** *pentroo sooveneeroorʸ*	
for the toilets	**pentru a merge la toaletă**	
	pentroo ah merjeh la twaleter	
Is it disabled-accessible?	**Există acces pentru persoane invalide?**	
	egzeester acches pentroo perswaneh eenvaleedeh	

For Tickets, see page 18.

Seeing the Sights

Where's...?	**Unde-i...?** *oondeʸ*	
the battleground	**câmpul de luptă** *cuhmpool deh loopter*	
the botanical garden	**grădina botanică**	
	grerdeena botaneecer	
the castle	**castelul** *castelool*	

the downtown	**centrul oraşului**
	chentrool oraşhoolooy
the fountain	**fântâna** *fuhntuhna*
the library	**biblioteca** *beeblee-oteca*
the market	**piaţă** *pyatser*
the museum	**muzeul** *mooze-ool*
the old town	**oraşul vechi** *oraşhool veky*
the opera house	**opera** *opera*
the palace	**palatul** *palatool*
the park	**parcul** *parcool*
the ruins	**ruinele** *roo-eeneleh*
the shopping area	**centrul comercial**
	chentrool comerchee-al
the town square	**piaţa oraşului** *pyatsah oraşhoolooy*
Can you show me	**Puteţi să-mi arătaţi pe hartă unde sunt?**
on the map?	*pootetsy sermy arertatsy peh harter oondeh soont*
It's...	**Este ...** *yesteh*
amazing	**uluitor** *ooloo-eetor*
beautiful	**frumos** *froomos*
boring	**plictisitor** *pleecteeseetor*
interesting	**interesant** *eenteresant*

magnificent	**magnific** *magneefeec*
romantic	**romantic** *romanteec*
strange	**straniu** *stranyoo*
terrible	**îngrozitor** *uhngrozeetor*
ugly	**urât** *ooruht*
I (don't) like it.	**Nu-mi place.** *noomy placheh*

For Asking Directions, see page 33.

Religious Sites

Where's…?	**Unde-i…?** *oondehy*
the cathedral	**catedrala** *catedrala*
the Catholic/	**biserică catolică/protestantă**
Protestant church	*beesereecer catoleecer/protestanter*
the mosque	**moschee** *moske-yeh*
the shrine	**altarul** *altarool*
the synagogue	**sinagogă** *seenagoger*
the temple	**templul** *templool*
What time is	**La ce oră este slujba?**
the service?	*la cheh orer yesteh sloozhba*

Shopping

ESSENTIAL

Where's the market/ mall?	**Unde-i o piaţă** *oondehy o pyatser*
I'm just looking.	**Mă uit doar.** *mer ooyt dwar*
Can you help me?	**Puteţi să mă ajutaţi?** *pootetsy ser mer azhootatsy*
I'm being helped.	**Sunt ajutat.** *Soont azhootat*
How much?	**Cât costă?** *cuht coster*
That one, please.	**acela, vă rog** *achela ver rog*
That's all.	**Asta-i tot.** *astay tot*
Where can I pay?	**Unde pot să plătesc** *Oonde pot ser plertesc*
I'll pay in cash/ by credit card.	**O să plătesc cu această carte de credit?** *o ser plertehsc coo achaster carteh deh credeet*
A receipt, please.	**Puteţi să-mi daţi, vă rog, o chitanţă?** *pootetsy sermy datsy ver rog o keetantser*

Opening hours vary. As a general rule, state-owned shops are open from 8:00a.m. until 8:00p.m., although some privately owned shops stay open around the clock. Department stores are open from 9.00a.m. until 8:00p.m. or 9:00p.m.
Food stores stay open on Saturdays and quite a few open on Sundays as well.

At the Shops

Where's. . .?	**Unde-i. . .?** *oondehy*
the antiques store	**un magazin de antichităţi** *oon magazeen deh anteekeetertsy*

the bakery	**o brutărie** *o brooter<u>ree</u>-eh*
the bank	**o bancă** *o <u>ban</u>cer*
the bookstore	**o librărie** *o leebrer<u>ree</u>-eh*
the clothing store	**magazinul de îmbrăcăminte** *maga<u>zee</u>nool deh uhmbrercer<u>meen</u>teh*
the delicatessen	**un magazin de delicatese** *oon maga<u>zeen</u> deh deleeca<u>te</u>seh*
the department	**un magazin universal** *oon maga<u>zeen</u> ooneever<u>sal</u>*
the gift shop	**magazinul de suveniruri** *maga<u>zee</u>nool deh soove<u>nee</u>roor^y*
the health food store	**magazinul cu produse alimentare sănătoase** *maga<u>zee</u>nool coo pro<u>doo</u>se aleemen<u>ta</u>reh sernert<u>wa</u>seh*
the jeweler	**un magazin de bijuterii** *oon maga<u>zeen</u> deh beezhootere<u>e</u>^y*
the liquor store [off-licence]	**un magazin de băuturi alcoolice** *oon maga<u>zeen</u> deh ba^{oo}toor^y alcohohleeche*
the market	**o piaţă** *o p^yatser*
the music store	**magazinul de muzică** *maga<u>zee</u>nool deh <u>moo</u>zeecer*
the pastry shop	**o plăcintărie** *o plercheenter<u>ree</u>-eh*
the pharmacy	**o farmacie** *o farma<u>chee</u>-eh*

the produce [grocery] store	**o băcănie** *o bercernee-eh*
the shoe store	**un magazin de încălțăminte** *oon magazeen deh uhncerltsermeenteh*
the shopping mall	**un centru comercial** *oon chentroo comerchee-al*
the souvenir store	**un magazin de suveniruri** *oon magazeen deh sooveneeroory*
the supermarket	**un magazin alimentar** *oon magazeen aleementar*
the tobacconist	**o tutungerie** *o tootoonjehree-eh*
the toy store	**un magazin de jucării** *oon magazeen deh zhoocer-reey*

Ask an Assistant

When do you open/close?	**Când se deschide/închide ...?** *cuhnd seh deskeedeh/uhnkeedeh*
the cashier	**casieria** *casee-ehree-ah*
the escalator	**escalatorul** *escalatorool*
the elevator [lift]	**liftul** *leeftool*
the fitting room	**cabina de probă?** *cabeena deh prober*
the store directory	**lista cu magazine** *leesta cu magazeeneh*
Can you help me?	**Puteți să mă ajutați?** *pootetsy ser mer azhootatsy*
I'm just looking.	**Mă uit doar.** *mer ooyt dwar*
I'm being helped.	**Sunt ajutat.** *Soont azhootat*
Do you have...?	**Aveți ...?** *avetsy*
Can you show me...?	**Puteți să-mi arătați ...?** *pootetsy sermy arertatsy*
Can you ship/wrap it?	**Vreți să-l împache tați?** *vretsy serl uhmpaketatsy*
How much?	**Cât costă?** *cuht coster*
That's all.	**Asta-i tot.** *astay tot*

For Clothing, see page 124.

For Souvenirs, see page 128.

YOU MAY HEAR...

Cu ce vă pot ajuta? *coo che ver pot ajoota*   Can I help you?
O clipă. *Oh cleeper.*   One moment.
Ce doriţi? *che doreetsy*   What would you like?
Mai doriţi ceva? *migh doreetsy cheeva*   Anything else?

YOU MAY SEE...

deschis/închis *deskees/uhnkees*	open/closed
închis pentru prânz *uhnkees pentroo pruhnz*	closed for lunch
cabină de probă *cabeener deh prober*	fitting room
casierie *casee-ehree-eh*	cashier
doar numerar *dwar noomerar*	cash only
se acceptă carduri de credit *seh akchepter cardoory deh credeet*	credit cards accepted
orar *orar*	business hours
** leşire** *yeschire*	exit

Personal Preferences

I'd like something...	**Aş vrea ceva...** *ash vreh-a cheva*
cheap/expensive	**ieftin/scump** *yefteen/scoomp*
larger/smaller	**mai mare/mai mic** *migh mareh/migh meec*
from this region	**din această regiune** *deen achaster regee-ooneh*
Around...euros.	**Aproximativ...euro.** *aproxeemateev... eh-ooroh*
Is it real?	**Este veritabil?** *yesteh vereetabeel*

Can you show me this/that?	**Puteţi să-mi arătaţi acesta/acela**
	pootetsy sermy arertatsy achesta/achela
That's not quite what I want.	**Nu este chiar ce vreau eu.**
	noo yesteh kyar cheh vreh-aoo yeoo
No, I don't like it.	**Nu-mi place.** *noomy placheh*
It's too expensive.	**E prea scump.** *yeh preh-a scoomp*
I have to think about it.	**Trebuie să mă mai gândesc.**
	trebooyeh ser mer migh guhndesc
I'll take it.	**Îl cumpăr.** *uhl coomperr*

Paying & Bargaining

How much?	**Cât costă?** *cuht coster*
I'll pay…	**Pot plăti cu …** *pot plertee coo*
in cash	**numerar** *noomerar*
by credit card	**cardul de credit?** *cardool deh credeet*
by traveler's check	**cec de călătorie?**
	chec deh cerlertoree-eh
A receipt, please.	**Puteţi să-mi daţi, vă rog, o chitanţă?**
	pootetsy sermy datsy ver rog o keetantser
That's too much.	**Costă prea mult.** *coster preh-a moolt*
I'll give you…	**Vă pot oferi…** *ver pot oferee…*
I have only…euros.	**Am doar… euro.** *am dwar eh-ooroh*
Is that your best price?	**Nu mai puteţi lăsa din preţ?**
	noo mai pootetsy lersah deen prets
Can you give me a discount?	**Îmi puteţi oferi o reducere?**
	uhmy pootetsy oferee oh redoochereh

For Numbers, see page 166.

YOU MAY HEAR...

Cum plătiți? *Coom plerteetsy?*

How are you paying?

Cartea dumneavoastră de credit a fost respinsă. *Carteh-a doomneh-avwastrer deh credeet a fost respeenser.*

Your credit card has been declined.

Buletinul, vă rog. *Booleteenool,ver rog*

ID, please.

Nu acceptăm carduri de credit. *Noo akchepterm cardoory deh credeet.*

We don't accept credit cards.

Doar numerar, vă rog. *Dwar noomerar, ver rog.*

Cash only, please.

Making a Complaint

I'd like...	**Aş vrea...** *ash vreh-a*
to exchange this	**să schimb aceasta** *ser skeemb achasta*
a refund	**banii înapoi** *baneey*
to see the manager	**să vorbesc cu şeful** *ser vorbesc coo shefool*

Services

Can you recommend...?	**Ne puteţi recomanda...?** *neh pootetsy recomanda*
a barber	**o frizerie** *o freezehree-eh*
a dry cleaner	**o curăţătorie** *o coorertsertoree-eh*
a hairstylist	**un salon de cosmetică** *oon salon deh cosmeteecer*
a Laundromat [launderette]	**o spălătorie/curăţătorie Nufărul** *o sperlertoree-eh/coorertsertoree-eh nooferrool*
a nail salon	**un salon de manichiură şi pedichiură** *oon salon deh maneekyoorer shee pedeekyoorer*
a spa	**un centru spa** *oon chentroo spa*
a travel agency	**o agenție de voiaj** *o ajentsee-eh deh voyazh*

Can you...this?	**Puteţi... asta ?** *pootetsy*
alter	**modifica** *modeefeeca*
clean	**pentru curăţa** *pentroo coorertsah*
fix	**repara** *repara*
press	**pentru călca** *pentroo cerlcat*
When will it be ready?	**Când va fi gata?** *cuhnd vah fee gata*

Hair & Beauty

I'd like...	**Aş vrea...** *ash vreh-a*
an appointment for today/tomorrow	**o programare pentru azi/mâine** *o programareh pentroo azy/muhyneh*
some color/ highlights	**o culoare/milaj** *o culware/meehladz*
my hair styled/ blow-dried	**o stilare/uscare** *o steelare-eh/uscare-eh*
a haircut	**o tunsoare** *o toonswareh*
an eyebrow/ bikini wax	**o epilare cu ceară a sprâncenelor/a zonei inghinale** *o ehpeelareh coo cheh-arer a spruhnchenelor/a zoney eengeenaleh*
a facial	**un tratament facial** *oon tratament fachee-al*

a manicure/ pedicure	**o manichiură** *o maneekyoorer*
a (sports) massage	**un masaj (sportiv)** *oon masazh (sporteev)*
A trim, please.	**Un tuns, vă rog.** *Oon toons, ver rog*
Not too short.	**Nu tundeți prea scurt.** *noo toondetsy preh-a scoort*
Shorter here.	**Puțin mai scurt.** *pootseen migh scoort*
Do you offer...?	**Oferiți servicii de...?** *Ofereetsy serveecheey deh...*
acupuncture	**acupunctură** *acooponctoorer*
aromatherapy	**aromaterapie** *aromaterapee-eh*
oxygen	**oxigenare** *oxeegenareh*
a sauna	**saună** *sa-ooner*

If you are interested in *objets d'art*, including icons on wood or glass, look for the shops belonging to the Artists' Union called **Fondul plastic**. There are many good contemporary art shops in Bucharest, notably Dominus (at the National Theatre).

Antiques

How old is it?	**Ce vechime are?** *Cheh vekeemeh areh*
Do you have anything from the...period?	**Aveți ceva obiecte din perioada...?** *Avetsy cheva obyecteh deen peree-wada...*
Do I have to fill out any forms?	**Trebuie să completez ceva formulare?** *Trebooyeh ser completez cheva formoolareh*
Is there a certificate of authenticity?	**Există un certificat de autenticitate?** *Egzeester oon cherteefeecat deh aootenteecheetateh*
Can you ship/wrap it?	**Vreți să-l împachetați?** *vretsy serl uhmpaketatsy*

Clothing

I'd like...	**Aş vrea...** *ash vreh-a*
Can I try this on?	**Pot să probez?** *pot ser probez*
It doesn't fit.	**Nu-mi vine bine.** *noom^y veeneh beeneh*
It's too...	**Este prea ...** *<u>yes</u>teh preh-a*
big/small	**mare/mic** *emareh/meec*
short/long	**scurt/lung** *scoort/loong*
tight/loose	**strâmt/larg** *struhmt/larg*
Do you have this in size...?	**Aveţi asta şi în mărimea...?** *Avets^y asta shee uhn mereemeh-a...*
Do you have this in a bigger/smaller size?	**Aveţi un număr mai mare/mic?** *Avets^y oon <u>noo</u>mer migh <u>ma</u>reh/<u>mee</u>c*

For Numbers, see page 166.

YOU MAY HEAR...

Vă stă foarte bine. *Ver ster <u>fwar</u>teh beeneh*	That looks great on you.
Cum vă vine? *<u>Coom</u> ver <u>vee</u>ne*	How does it fit?
Nu avem mărimea dumneavoastră. *Noo <u>a</u>vem me<u>ree</u>me-ah doomneh-a<u>vwa</u>strer*	We don't have your size.

YOU MAY SEE...

bărbaţi *ber-r<u>bats</u>^y*	men's
femei *feme^y*	women's
copii *cope^y*	children's

Colors

I'd like something...	**Aş vrea ceva în ...**	*ash vreh-a cheva uhn*
beige	**bej** *bezh*	
black	**negru** *negroo*	
blue	**albastru** *albastroo*	
brown	**maro** *maro*	
green	**verde** *verdeh*	
gray	**gri** *gree*	
orange	**portocaliu** *portocalee⁰⁰*	
pink	**roz** *roz*	
purple	**roşu-închis (purpuriu)** *roshu-uhnkees (poorpooree⁰⁰)*	
red	**roşu** *roshoo*	
white	**alb** *alb*	
yellow	**galben** *galben*	

Clothes & Accessories

a backpack	**un rucsac** *oon roocsac*
a belt	**curea** *cooreh-a*
a bikini	**o pereche de bikini** *o perekeh de beekeenee*
a blouse	**o bluză** *o bloozer*
a bra	**un sutien** *oon sootee-en*
briefs [underpants]/ panties	**nişte chiloţi/ chiloţi** *keelotsy/ neeshteh keelotsy*
a coat	**o haină** *o hayner*
a dress	**o rochie** *o rokee-eh*
a hat	**o pălărie** *o perlerree-eh*
a jacket	**o jachetă** *o zhaketer*
jeans	**nişte blugi** *neeshteh bloojy*
pajamas	**o pijamă** *o peezhamer*
pants [trousers]	**pantaloni/nişte pantaloni** *pantalony/neeshteh pantalony*

pantyhose [tights]	**ciorapi cu chilot/nişte dresuri** _chorapy coo keelot/neeshteh dresoory_
a purse [handbag]	**o geantă** _o janter_
a raincoat	**o haină de ploaie** _o hayner deh plwayeh_
a scarf	**un fular** _oon foolar_
a shirt	**o cămaşă** _o cermasher_
shorts	**şortici** _shortychy_
a skirt	**o fustă** _o fooster_
socks	**nişte şosete** _neeshteh shoseteh_
a suit	**un costum bărbătesc/un costum de damă** _oon costoom berrbertesc/oon costoom deh damer_
sunglasses	**ochelari de soare** _okelary deh swareh_
a sweater	**un pulover** _oon poolover_
a sweatshirt	**o bluză de trening din bumbac** _o bloozer deh treneeng deen boombac_
a swimsuit	**un costum de înot** _oon costoom deh uhnot_
a T-shirt	**o cămaşă** _o cermasher_
a tie	**o cravată** _o cravater_
underwear	**lenjerie intimă** _lenzheree-eh eenteemer_

Fabric

I'd like…	**Aş vrea…** *ash vreh-a*
cotton	**bumbac** *boombac*
denim	**doc** *doc*
lace	**dantelă** *danteler*
leather	**piele** *pyeleh*
linen	**in** *een*
silk	**mătase** *mertaseh*
wool	**lână** *luhner*

Is it machine washable? **Se spală la maşină?** *seh spaler la masheener*

Shoes

I'd like…	**Aş vrea…** *ash vreh-a*
high-heels/flats	**cu tocuri/plaţi** *coo tocoory/platsy*
boots	**cizme** *cheezmeh*
loafers	**mocasini** *mocaseeny*
sandals	**sandale** *sandaleh*
shoes	**pantofi** *pantofy*
slippers	**papuci** *papoochy*
sneakers	**tenişi** *teneeshy*
Size…	**Măsura…** *mersoora*

For Numbers, see page 166.

Sizes can vary somewhat from one manufacturer to another, so
be sure to try on shoes and clothing before you buy.

Sizes

small (S)	**mic**	_meec_
medium (M)	**mediu**	_medy^{oo}_
large (L)	**mare**	_mareh_
extra large (XL)	**XL**	_eex-ehl_
petite	**minionă**	_meenyoner_
plus size	**XXL**	_eex-eex-ehl_

Newsagent & Tobacconist

Do you sell English-language newspapers?	**Vindeţi ziare în limba engleză?** _Veendetsy zee-areh uhn leembah ehnglezer_	
I'd like...	**Aş vrea...** _ash vreh-a_	
candy [sweets]	**nişte dropsuri/nişte dulciuri** _neeshteh dropsoory/neeshteh doolchoory_	
chewing gum	**nişte gumă de mestecat** _neeshteh goomer deh mestecat_	
a chocolate bar	**ciocolată** _chocolater_	
a cigar	**trabuc** _trabooc_	
a pack/carton of cigarettes	**nişte ţigări** _neeshteh tseegerry_	
a lighter	**o brichetă** _o breeketer_	
a magazine	**o revistă** _o reveester_	
matches	**nişte chibrituri** _neeshteh keebreetoory_	
a newspaper	**ziar** _zee-ar_	
a pen	**un stilou** _oon steelo^{oo}_	
a postcard	**o vedere** _o vedereh_	

a road/town map of...	**o hartă a drumurilor naţionale...**
	o harta a droomooreelor natsee-onaleh...
stamps	**nişte timbre** *neeshteh teembreh*

Romania has a few English-language newspapers, both the *Nine O'Clock* (www.nineoclock.ro), and the *Romania Business Insider* (www.romania-insider.com) have online versions.

Photography

I'd like...camera.	**Aş vrea un aparat de fotografiat ...**
	ash vreh-a oon aparat deh fotografeeat...
an automatic	**automat** *a-ootomat*
a digital	**digital** *deejeetal*
a disposable	**de unică folosinţă** *deh ooneecer foloseentser*
I'd like...	**Aş vrea...** *ash vreh-a...*
a battery	**baterie** *o bateree-eh*
digital prints	**fotografii digitale** *fotografeey deegeetaleh*
a memory card	**card de memorie** *card de memoree-e*
Can I print digital photos here?	**Pot fi imprimate aici fotografii digitale?**
	Pot fee eempreemateh a-eechy fotografeey deegeetaleh

Souvenirs

an art book	**album de artă** *alboom deh arter*
a bottle of wine	**o sticlă de vin** *o steecler deh veen*
a box of chocolates	**o cutie de bomboane de ciocolată**
	o cootee-eh deh bom-bwaneh deh chocolater
a carpet	**carpetă** *carpeter*
ceramics	**ceramică** *cherameeker*
some crystal	**cristal** *creestal*

a doll	**o păpuşă** *o perpoosher*
an icon	**icoană** *eekwaner*
some jewelry	**nişte bijuterii** *neeshteh beezhooteree^y*
a key ring	**un breloc** *oon breloc*
a postcard	**o vedere** *o vedereh*
a painting	**tablou/pictură** *tabloo/pictoorer*
some pottery	**olărit** *olerreet*
a T-shirt	**o cămaşă** *o cermasher*
a tablecloth	**faţă de masă** *fatser der maser*
a tapestry	**tapiserie** *tapeeseree-eh*
a toy	**jucărie** *zhoocerree-eh*
a wooden utensil	**unelte de lemn** *oonelteh deh lemn*
Can I see this/that?	**Îmi puteţi arăta asta/aceea?**
	Uhm pootets^y arerta asta/acheh-eh-a
I'd like...	**Aş vrea...** *ash vreh-a*
a battery	**o baterie** *o bateree-eh*
a bracelet	**o brăţară** *o brertsarer*
a brooch	**o broşă** *o brosher*
a clock	**un ceas** *oon chas*
earrings	**nişte cercei** *neeshteh chercheh^y*
a necklace	**un colier** *oon colee-er*

a ring	**un inel** *oon eenel*
a watch	**un ceas** *oon chas*
I'd like...	**Aş vrea...** *ash vreh-a...*
copper	**cupru** *cooproo*
crystal	**cristal** *creestal*
diamonds	**diamant** *deeamant*
white/yellow gold	**aur** *a-oor*
pearls	**perlă** *perler*
pewter	**aliaj pe bază de cositor**
	alee-azh peh bazer deh coseetor
platinum	**platină** *plateener*
sterling silver	**argint** *arjeent*
Is this real?	**Este veritabil?**
	yesteh vereetabeel
Can you engrave it?	**O puteţi grava?**
	O pootetsy grava

Shops called **artizanat** sell typical Romanian souvenirs
including finely embroidered tunics, blouses, napkins, tablecloths
and headscarves. You'll also find traditional woollen carpets
handwoven with intricate geometric patterns, hand-painted Easter
eggs, decorative pottery and beautiful, carved wooden utensils.
A bottle of Romanian plum brandy (**ţuică**) or a catalogue of medieval
art, and of course some Romanian folk or classical music, all make good
souvenirs of the country.

Sport & Leisure

ESSENTIAL

When's the game?	**Când este jocul?** *Cuhnd yesteh zhocool*
Where's...?	**Unde este...?** *oondeh yesteh*
the beach	**plajă** *plazher*
the park	**parcul** *parcool*
the pool	**piscină** *pees-cheener*
Is it safe to swim here?	**Se poate înota în siguranţă aici?**
	Seh pwateh uhnota seegoorantser a-eechy
Can I hire clubs?	**Pot să închiriez crose de golf?**
	Pot ser uhnkeeree-ehz croseh deh golf
How much per	**Cât costă o oră/zi de folosire?**
hour/day?	*cuht coster o orer/zee deh foloseere*
How far is it to...?	**Este departe până la ...?**
	yesteh departeh puhner la
Show me on the map,	**Puteţi să-mi arătaţi pe hartă.**
please.	*pootetsy sermy arertatsy peh harter*

Watching Sport

When's...(game/	**Când se începe (jocul/cursa/campionatul) de...?**
race/tournament)?	*Cuhnd seh uhnchepeh (zhocool/coorsa/campionatool)*
	deh...
the baseball	**baseball** *beysbol*
the basketball	**baschet** *basket*
the boxing	**box** *box*
the cricket	**crichet** *creeket*
the cycling	**ciclism** *cheecleesm*
the golf	**golf** *golf*

the soccer [football]	**fotbal** _fotbal_	
the tennis	**tenis** _tenees_	
the volleyball	**voleibal** _voleybal_	
Who's playing?	**Cine joacă?** _Cheeneh zhwacer_	
Where's the racetrack/ stadium?	**Unde este stadionul?** _oondeh yesteh stadee-onool_	
Where can I place a bet?	**Unde pot să pariez?** _Oondeh pot ser paree-ehz_	

Playing Sport

Where is/are . . .?	**Unde este/sunt . . .?** _oondeh yesteh/soont..._	
the golf course	**Unde este terenul de golf cel mai apropiat?** _oondeh yesteh terenool deh golf chel migh apropee-at_	
the gym	**sala de sport** _sala deh sport_	
the park	**parcul** _parcool_	
the tennis courts	**Unde se află terenurile de tenis?** _oondeh seh afler terenooreeleh deh tenees_	
How much per. . .	**Cât costă pe . . .?** _cuht coster peh_	
day	**zi** _zee_	
hour	**oră** _orer_	
game	**joc** _joc_	
round	**meci** _mechy_	
Can I rent [hire]. . .?	**Pot să închiriez . . .?** _pot ser uhnkeeree-ez_	
some clubs	**crose de golf** _croseh deh golf_	
some equipment	**echipament** _ekipament_	
a racket	**rachete de tennis** _raketeh deh tenees_	

At the Beach/Pool

Where's the beach/ pool?	**Unde este plaja/piscina?** _Oondeh yesteh plazhah/peescheena_	
Is there a. . .?	**Există o . . .** _egzeester o . . ._	
kiddie pool	**piscină pentru copii** _peescheener pentroo copeey_	
indoor/outdoor	**piscină interioară/exterioară**	

pool	*peescheener eentereewarer/ehxtereewarer*
lifeguard	**Există salvamar?** *egzeester salvamar*
Is it safe…?	**Se poate…?** *se pwateh*
to swim	**înota** *uhnota*
to dive	**sări în apă** *ser-ree uhn aper*
for children	**Nu este periculos pentru copii?**
	noo yesteh pereecoolos pentroo copeey
I'd like to hire…	**Vreau să închiriez…** *vraoo ser uhnkeeree-ez*
a deck chair	**un şezlong** *oon shezlong*
diving equipment	**un echipament de plonjat**
	oon ekeepament deh plonzhat
a jet ski	**un ski-jet** *oon skee-zhet*
a motorboat	**o barcă cu motor** *o barcer coo motor*
a rowboat	**o barcă cu rame** *o barcer coo rameh*
snorkeling	**un echipament pentru scufundări**
equipment	*oon ekipament pentroo scoofoondery*
a surfboard	**un acuaplan/o planşă de surf**
	oon acwaplan/o plansher deh surf
a towel	**un prosop** *oon prosop*
an umbrella	**o umbrelă** *o oombreler*
water skis	**nişte schiuri nautice** *neeshteh skeeoory naooteecheh*

| a windsurfing board | **o placă de windsurfing** *o placer deh weendserfeeng* |
| For…hours. | **Pentru…ore.** *Pentroo… oreh* |

Skiing is popular in Romania thanks to the country's mountaineous regions. The most well-known resorts are Poiana Braşov, Sinaia and Predeal. Weekend crowds can be big however, and queues for the cable cars can take up to a few hours.

Winter Sports

A lift pass for a day/five days, please.	**Un abonament de ski pentru o zi/cinci zile, vă rog.** *Oon abonament deh skee pentroo o zee/cheenchy zeeleh, ver rog.*
I'd like to hire…	**Vreau să închiriez…** *vraoo ser uhnkeeree-ez*
boots	**cizme** *cheezmeh*
a helmet	**o cască** *oh cascer*
poles	**o prăjină** *o prerzheener*
skis	**nişte schiuri** *neeshteh skeeoory*
a snowboard	**un snowboard** *oon snowboard*
snowshoes	**rachete de zăpadă** *raketeh deh zerpader*
These are too big/small.	**Aceştia sunt mari/mici.** *acheshtya soont mary/meechy*
Are there lessons?	**Sunt lecţii?** *soont lectseey*
I'm a beginner.	**Sunt începător.** *soont uhnchepertor*
I'm experienced.	**Sunt experimentat.** *soont expereementat*
A trail map, please.	**O hartă de traseu, vă rog.** *o harter de traseoo ver rog*

YOU MAY SEE...

lifturi *leeftoory*	lifts
teleschi *teleskee*	drag lift
teleferic *telefereec*	cable car
telescaun *telescah-oon*	chair lift
începători *uhnchepertory*	novice
nivel mediu *neevel medyoo*	intermediate
avansaţi *avansatsy*	expert
pârtie închisă *puhrtee-eh uhnkeeser*	trail [piste] closed

Out in the Country

A map of..., please.	**o hartă de...** *o harter deh*
this region	**această regiune** *achaster regee-ooneh*
the walking routes	**trasee de mers pe jos** *traseh-eh deh mers peh zhos*
the bike routes	**trasee pentru biciclete**
	traseh-eh pentroo beecheecleteh
the trails	**poteci** *potechy*
Is it...?	**Este ...?** *yesteh...*
easy	**uşor** *uschor*
difficult	**greu** *greoo*

far	**departe** _departeh_
steep	**abrupt** _abroopt_
How far is it to…?	**Este departe până la …?** _yesteh departeh puhner la_
I'm lost.	**M-am rătăcit** _mam rertercheet_
Where's…?	**Unde este …?** _oondeh yesteh_
the bridge	**pod** _pod_
the cave	**peştera** _peshtera_
the desert	**deşertul** _deshertool_
the farm	**fermă** _fermer_
the field	**câmp** _cuhmp_
the forest	**pădure** _perdooreh_
the hill	**deal** _dal_
the lake	**lac** _lac_
the mountain	**munte** _moonteh_
the nature preserve	**rezervaţia naturală** _rezervatsee-a natooraler_
the viewpoint	**punctul de observaţie** _poonctool deh obervatsee-eh_
the park	**parcul** _parcool_
the path	**potecă** _potecer_
the peak	**vârf** _vuhrf_
the picnic area	**zona pentru picnic** _zonah pentroo peecneec_
the pond	**iaz** _yaz_
the river	**râu** _ruhoo_
the sea	**mare** _mareh_
the (hot) spring	**izvor** _eezvor_
the stream	**pârâul** _puhruh-ool_
the valley	**vale** _valeh_
the vineyard	**vie** _vee-eh_
the waterfall	**cascadă** _cascader_

ESSENTIAL

What's there to do at night?	**Ce se poate face noaptea?** *Cheh seh pwateh facheh nwapteh-a?*
Do you have a program of events?	**Aveți un program al evenimentelor?** *Avetsy oon program al eveneementelor*
What's playing tonight?	**Ce rulează în seara asta?** *Cheh rooleh-azer uhn seh-ara asta*
Where's...?	**Unde este...** *oondeh ehsteh*
the downtown area	**zona centrală** *zona centraler*
the bar	**barul** *barool*
the dance club	**discoteca** *deescoteca*

Entertainment

Can you recommend...?	**Puteți recomanda ...?** *pootetsy recomanda...*
a concert	**un concert** *oon conchert*
a movie	**film** *film*
an opera	**o operă** *o operer*
a play	**o piesă** *o pieser*
When does it start/ end?	**La ce oră se începe spectacolul?** *la cheh orer seh uhnchepeh spectacolool*
What's the dress code?	**Care este codul vestimentar?** *Careh yesteh codool vesteementar*
I like...	**Aș vrea ...** *ash vreh-a*
classical music	**muzică clasică** *moozeecer claseecer*
folk music	**muzică populară** *moozeecer popoolarer*

jazz	**jazz** *jazz*
pop music	**muzică pop** _moo_zeecer pop
rap	**rap** *rap*

For Tickets, see page 18.

YOU MAY HEAR...

Închideţi-vă telefoanele mobile, vă rog.
Uhn_kee_detseever telef_wa_neleh mo_bee_leh, ver rog.

Turn off your mobile phones, please.

Nightlife

What's there to do at night?	**Ce se poate face noaptea?**
	Cheh seh _pwa_teh _fa_cheh n_wap_teh-a
Can you recommend...?	**Puteţi recomanda ...?**
	poo_tet_sy recoman_da_
a bar	**un bar** *oon _bar_*
a cabaret	**un cabaret** *oon cabar_et_*
a casino	**un cazinou** *oon cazee_no_ºº*
a dance club	**o discotecă**
	oh deesco_te_cer
a gay club	**un club pentru homosexuali**
	oon cloob _pen_troo homosex_ooal_y
a jazz club	**un club de jaz** *oon cloob deh _jaz_*
a club with French music	**un club cu muzică franceză**
	oon cloob coo _moo_zeecer franchezer
Is there live music?	**Se cântă live?** *Seh _cuhn_ter _ligh_v*
How do I get there?	**Cum se ajunge acolo?**
	coom seh a_zhoon_jeh a_co_lo

Is there a cover charge?	**Cât costă?** *cuht coster*
Let's go dancing.	**Să mergem să dansăm.** *Seh merjem seh danserm*
Is this area safe at night?	**Este sigură această zonă pe timpul nopţii?** *Yesteh seegoorer achaster zoner uhn teempool noptsee*

Special Requirements

ESSENTIAL

I'm here on business.	**Sunt/Am venit în interes de serviciu.** _soont/am veneet uhn eenteres deh_
Here's my card.	**Poftiţi cartea mea de vizită.** _pofteetsy carteh-a meh-a deh veezeeter_
Can I have your card?	**Îmi puteţi da cartea dumneavoastră de vizită?** _uhmy pootetsy da carteh-a doomneh-avwastrer deh veezeeter_
I have a meeting with...	**Am o întâlnire cu...** _am oh uhntuhlneereh coo..._
Where's...?	**Unde este...?** _oondeh yesteh..._
the business center	**centrul de afaceri** _chentrool deh afachery_
the convention hall	**sala de conferinţe** _sala deh confereentseh_
the meeting room	**sala de şedinţe** _sala deh shedeentseh_

A handshake with direct eye contact is the customary greeting for business people. People are addressed by **Domnul** for Mr. and **Doamna** for Mrs., followed by their surname.

On Business

I'm here for...	**Sunt aici pentru...** _soont a-eechy pentroo..._
a seminar	**un seminar** _oon semeenar_
a conference	**o conferinţă** _o confereentser_
a meeting	**o întâlnire** _o uhntuhlneereh_

My name is...	**Mă numesc...**	
	Mer noomehsc	
May I introduce	**Daţi-mi voie să vă prezint pe...?**	
my colleague...	*datseemy voyeh ser ver prezeent peh colegul meu...*	
I have a meeting/an	**Am o întâlnire cu...**	
appointment with...	*am o uhntuhl-neereh coo*	
I'm sorry I'm late.	**Îmi cer scuze pentru întârziere.**	
	uhmy cher scoozeh pentroo uhntuhrzee-ehreh.	
I need an interpreter.	**Am nevoie de un traducător.**	
	am nevoyeh deh oon tradoocertor	
You can contact	**Mă puteţi contacta la Hotelul ...**	
me at the...Hotel.	*mer pootetsy contacta la Hotelool...*	
I'm here until...	**Sunt aici până...**	
	soont a-eechy puhner	
I need to...		
make a call	**Aş vrea să telefonez la numărul...**	
	ash vreh-a ser telefonez la noomerrool...	
make a photocopy	**să fac o fotocopie**	
	ser fac o fotocopee-eh	
send an e-mail	**să trimit un e-mail**	
	ser treemeet oon ee-mayl	

send a fax	**Aş dori să trimit un fax**
	ash doree ser tree<u>meet</u> un fax
send a package	**să trimit un colet (să ajungă a doua zi)**
(for next-day	*ser tree<u>meet</u> oon colet (ser a<u>zhoon</u>ger a <u>do</u>-wa <u>zee</u>)*
delivery)	
It was a pleasure	**Mi-a făcut plăcere să vă cunosc.**
to meet you.	*mee-ah fer<u>coot</u> pler<u>cher</u>eh ser ver coo<u>nosc</u>*

For Communications, see page 48.

YOU MAY HEAR...

Aveţi o programare?	Do you have an
a<u>vets</u>y o progra<u>ma</u>reh	appointment?
Cu cine? *coo <u>chee</u>neh*	With whom?
Este într-o şedinţă.	He/She is in a meeting.
yesteh uhntroh she<u>deen</u>tser	
Un moment, vă rog. *oon moment ver rog*	One moment, please.
Luaţi loc. *<u>lwats</u>y loc*	Have a seat.
Ce doriţi să beţi?	Would you like something
che do<u>ree</u>tee ser be<u>tsee</u>	to drink?
Vă mulţumesc de vizită.	Thank you for coming.
ver mooltsoo<u>mesc</u> deh veezeeter	

Traveling With Children

ESSENTIAL

Is there a discount for kids?	**Oferiţi reduceri pentru copii?**
	Ofereetsy redoochery pentroo copeey
Can you recommend a babysitter?	**Îmi puteţi recomanda o baby sitter?**
	Uhmy pootetsy recomanda o babyseeter
Do you have a child's seat/highchair?	**Aveţi un scaun pentru copii?**
	Avetsy oon scaoon pentroo copeey
Where can I change the baby?	**Unde aş putea schimba copilul?**
	Oondeh ash pooteh-a skeembah copeelool

Out & About

Can you recommend something for kids?	**Îmi puteţi recomanda ceva pentru copii?**
	uhmy pootetsy recomanda cheva pentroo copeey
Where's…?	**Unde este/sunt …?** *oondeh yesteh/soont*
the amusement park	**parcul de distracţii**
	parcool deh deestractseey
the arcade	**jocurile mecanice**
	zhocooreeleh mecaneecheh
the kiddie [paddling] pool	**bazinul pentru copii**
	bazeenool pentroo copeey
the park	**parcul** *parcool*
the playground	**teren de joacă** *teren de zhwacer*
the zoo	**grădina zoologică** *grerdeena zo-olojeecer*
Are kids allowed?	**Se poate cu copiii aici?**
	Ser pwate coo copee-eey a-eechy

Is it safe for kids?	**Nu este periculos pentru copii?**
	noo <u>yes</u>teh pereecoo<u>los</u> <u>pen</u>troo co<u>pee</u>^y
Is it suitable for	**Se potriveşte şi pentru copiii de...**
...year olds?	*seh potree<u>veh</u>shteh shee <u>pehn</u>troo co<u>pee</u>eey deh...*

For Numbers, see page 166.

YOU MAY HEAR...

Cum vă numiţi?	How cute! What's
coom ver noo<u>meets</u>^y	his/her name?
Ce vârstă aveţi?/Câţi ani ai?	How old is he/she?
cheh <u>vuhr</u>ster a<u>vets</u>^y/<u>cuhts</u>^y any igh	

Baby Essentials

Do you have...?	**Aveţi ...?** *avets^y*
a baby bottle	**un biberon** *oon beeberon*
baby food	**alimente pentru copii**
	aleementeh <u>pen</u>troo co<u>pee</u>^y
baby wipes	**şerveţele pentru copii** *shervetseleh <u>pen</u>troo co<u>pee</u>^y*

a car seat	**un scaun auto pentru copii**
	oon scaoon a-ootoh pentroo copee^y
a children's menu/portion	**un meniu/o porţie pentru copii**
	oon menee^{oo}/o portsee-eh pentroo copee^y
a child's seat/ highchair	**un scaun de masă pentru copii**
	oon scaoon deh maser pentroo copee
a crib/cot	**un pătuţ** *oon pertoots*
diapers [nappies]	**scutece de unică folosinţă**
	scootecheh deh ooneecer foloseentser
formula	**lapte praf** *lapteh praf*
a pacifier [dummy]	**o suzetă** *o soozeter*
a playpen	**un ţarc pentru copii**
	oon tsarc pentroo copee^y
a stroller [pushchair]	**un cărucior** *oon cer-roochor*
Can I breastfeed the baby here?	**Pot alăpta bebeluşul aici?**
	Pot alerpta bebelooshool a-eech^y
Where can I breastfeed/change the baby?	**Unde aş putea alăpta/schimba bebeluşul?**
	Oonde ash pooteh-a alerpta/skeemba bebelooshool

For Dining with Children, see page 63.

Babysitting

Can you recommend a babysitter?	**Îmi puteţi recomanda o baby sitter?**
	Uhmy pootetsy recomanda o babyseeter
How much do you/ they charge?	**Cât o să mă coste?**
	Cuht o ser mer costeh
I'll be back at...	**O să revin la ...**
	Oh ser reveen la...
If you need to contact me, call...	**Dacă va fi nevoie să mă contactezi, sună la...**
	Dacer va fee nevoyeh ser mer contactezy, sooner la...

For Time, see page 168.

Health & Emergency

Can you recommend a pediatrician?	**Îmi puteţi recomanda un pediatru?**
	Uhmy pootetsy recomanda oon pedeeatroo
My child is allergic to...	**Copilul meu este alergic la...**
	Copeelool meoo yesteh alergeec la...
My child is missing.	**Copilul meu s-a pierdut.**
	Copeelool meoo sa pyerdoot
Have you seen a boy/girl?	**Aţi văzut un băiat/o fată?**
	Atsy verzoot oon beryat/o fater

For Health, see page 153.

For Police, see page 151.

Disabled Travelers

ESSENTIAL

Is there...?	**Este/Există...?**	_yesteh/egzeester_
access for the disabled	**Există acces pentru persoane invalide?** _egzeester acches pentroo perswaneh eenvaleedeh_	
a wheelchair ramp	**o rampă pentru scaune cu rotile** _o ramper pentroo scaooneh coo roteeleh_	
a disabled-accessible toilet	**o toaletă pentru persoane cu handicap** _o twaleter pentroo pehrswaneh coo handeecap_	
I need...	**Am nevoie de ...** _am nevoyeh deh_	
assistance	**ajutor** _azhootor_	
an elevator [a lift]	**liftul** _leeftool_	
a ground-floor room	**o cameră la parter** _o camerer la partehr_	

Asking for Assistance

I'm...	**Sunt...** _soont_	
disabled	**persoană invalidă** _perswaner eenvaleeder_	
visually impaired	**o persoană cu deficienţe de vedere** _o pehrswaner coo defeechee-ehntseh deh vedereh_	
deaf	**surd** _soord_	
hearing impaired	**o persoană cu deficienţe de auz** _o pehrswaner coo defeechee-ehntseh deh aooz_	
unable to walk far/ use the stairs	**Nu pot să merg pe distanţe mari/să folosesc scările** _Noo pot ser merg peh deestantseh mary/ser folosesc scer-reeleh_	
Please speak louder.	**Vorbiţi mai tare, vă rog.** _vorbeetsy migh tareh ver rog_	

Can I bring my wheelchair?	**Pot să îmi aduc scaunul cu rotile?**
	Pot ser uhm^y adooc scaoonool coo roteeleh
Are guide dogs permitted?	**Este permis accesul cu câine-ghid?**
	Yesteh permees akchesool coo cuhyneh-geed
Can you help me?	**Puteţi să mă ajutaţi?** *pootets^y ser mer azhootats^y*
Please open/ hold the door.	**Vă rog deschideţi/ţineţi uşa.**
	Ver rog deskeedets^y/tseenets^y oosha.

For Health, see page 153.

In an Emergency

Emergencies

ESSENTIAL

Help!	**Ajutor!** *ajootor*
Go away!	**Pleacă de aici!** *pleh-acer deh a-<u>eech</u>y*
Stop, thief!	**Stop, hoţul!** *stop hotsool*
Get a doctor!	**Chemaţi un doctor!** *kematsy oon doctor*
Fire!	**Foc!** *foc*
I'm lost.	**M-am rătăcit.** *mam rertercheet*
Can you help me?	**Puteţi să mă ajutaţi?** *poot<u>ets</u>y ser mer azhootatsy*
Police!	**Poliţia!** *pol<u>eet</u>see-a*

Police

ESSENTIAL

Call the police!	**Chemaţi poliţia** *k<u>emats</u>y pol<u>eet</u>see-a*
Where's the police station?	**Unde este un post de poliţie?** *oondeh yesteh oon post deh pol<u>eet</u>see-eh*
There was an accident/attack.	**A fost un accident.** *a fost oon acch<u>ee</u>dent*
My child is missing.	**Copilul meu s-a pierdut.** *cop<u>ee</u>lool <u>me</u>oo sa pyerdoot*
I need...	**Am nevoie...** *am nevoyeh...*
an interpreter	**de un interpret** *deh oon interpret*
to make a phone call.	**să dau un telefon.** *ser <u>da</u>oo oon tel<u>efon</u>*
I'm innocent.	**Sunt nevinovat.** *<u>soont</u> neveeno<u>vat</u>*

Driving at night is not advised as roads are poorly lit and cyclists and horse carts frequently travel without adequate lights. The wearing of seatbelts is compulsory, and driving with any alcohol in the bloodstream is prohibited.

Crime & Lost Property

I want to report...	**Vreau să raportez**	vreh-aoo ser rapor_tez_
a mugging	**o tâlhărie**	o tuhlher-ree-eh
a rape	**un viol**	oon _vyol_
a theft	**un furt**	oon foort
I was mugged.	**Am fost tâlhărit.**	am _fost_ tuhlher-_reet_
I was robbed.	**Am fost jefuit.**	am _fost_ zhefoo-_eet_
I lost...	**Am pierdut ...**	am pᵞerdoot...
...was stolen.	**Mi s-a furat ...**	mee sa foo_rat_...
My backpack	**un rucsac**	oon _roo_csac
My bicycle	**bicicletă**	beecheecleter
My camera	**aparatul foto**	apartool foto
My (hire) car	**maşina (închiriată)**	ma_shee_na (uhnkeer-ee-_ah_ter)
My computer	**un computer**	oon com_pyoo_ter
My credit card	**cartea de credit**	carteh-a deh _cre_deet
My jewelry	**Bijuteriile**	beezhooter_ee-ee_-leh
My money	**bani**	banᵞ
My passport	**paşaportul**	pashap_or_tool
My purse [handbag]	**poşeta/geanta**	po_she_ta//jeh-anta
My traveler's cheques	**cecurile de călătorie**	checooreeleh deh cerlerto_ree_-eh
My wallet	**portmoneul**	portmon_e_-ool
I need a police report.	**Vreau să depun o plângere la poliţie.**	vreh-aoo ser depoon o pluhnjereh la po_leet_see-eh

| Where is the British/ American/Irish embassy? | **Unde este ambasada britanică/ americană/ irlandeză?** *oondeh yesteh ambasader breetaneecer/ amereecaner / irlandezer* |

Health

ESSENTIAL

I'm sick.	**Sunt bolnav.** *soont bolnav*
I need an English-speaking doctor.	**Unde pot găsi un doctor care vorbește englezește?** *oondeh pot gersee oon doctor careh vorbeshteh englezeshteh*
It hurts here.	**Mă doare aici.** *mer dwareh a-eechy.*

Finding a Doctor

Can you recommend a doctor/dentist?	**Îmi puteți recomanda un doctor/dentist?** *uhmy pootetsy recomanda oon doctor/dentist*
Can the doctor come here?	**Poate doctorul să vină să mă vadă aici?** *pwateh doctorool ser veener ser mer vader a-eechy*
I need an English-speaking doctor.	**Unde pot găsi un doctor care vorbește englezește?** *oondeh pot gersee oon doctor careh vorbeshteh englezeshteh*
What are the office hours?	**Care sunt orele de program?** *careh soont oreleh deh program*
I'd like an appointment for...	**Vreau să-mi fac o programare la doctor pentru...** *vraoo sermy fac o programare la doctor pentroo... veezeeter la doctor*
today	**azi** *azy*
tomorrow	**mâine** *muhyneh*

If you fall ill during your stay in Romania, ask for a **policlinică cu plată** (paying clinic); these are relatively inexpensive and can give you immediate attention by very good doctors.
For minor complaints you can get advice from any pharmacy.

as soon as possible	**cât de curând posibil** *cuht deh cooruhnd poseebeel*
It's urgent.	**Este urgent.** *yesteh oorgent*

Symptoms

I'm bleeding.	**Sângerează.** *suhnjerazer*
I'm constipated.	**Sunt constipat.** *soont consteepat*
I'm dizzy.	**Sunt ameţit** m/**ameţită** f. *ametseet/ametseeter*
I'm nauseous.	**mi-e greaţă** *myeh gratser*
I'm vomiting.	**Am vărsat.** *am verrsat*
It hurts here.	**Mă doare aici.** *mer dwareh a-eechy*
I have...	**Am ...** *Am...*
cramps	**crampe** *crampeh*
diarrhea	**diaree** *dee-are-eh*
an earache	**o durere de ureche** *o doorereh deh oorekeh*
a fever	**febră** *febrer*
pain	**dureri** *doorery*
a rash	**o eczemă** *o egzemer*
a sprain	**o luxaţie** *looxatsye*
some swelling	**o umflătură** *o oomflertoorer*
a sore throat	**o durere în gât** *o doorereh uhn guht*
a stomachache	**o durere de burtă** *o doorereh deh boorter*
I have an allergic reaction.	**Am o reacţie alergică.** *am o reactsee alerjeecer*
I have chest pain.	**Mă doare pieptul.** *mer dwareh pyeptool*

I've been sick for...days.	**Sunt bolnav** *m*/**bolnavă** *f* **de... zile.** *soont bolnav / bolnaver deh ... seeleh*

For Numbers, see page 166.

Conditions

I'm...	**Sunt...** *soont*
anemic	**anemic** *m*/**anemică** *f* *anemeec / anemeecer*
asthmatic	**astmatic** *m*/**astmatică** *f* *astmateec / astmateecer*
diabetic	**diabetic** *m*/**diabetică** *f*
	soont dee-abeteec/dee-abeteecer
epileptic	**epileptic** *m*/**epileptică** *f* *epeelepteec/ epeelepteecer*
I'm allergic to antibiotics/penicillin.	**Sunt alergic** *m*/**alergică** *f* **la antibiotice/penicilină.** *soont alerjeec/ alerjeecer la anoomeeteh anteebee-oteecheh/peneecheeleener*
I have...	**Am ...** *am*
arthritis	**artrită** *artreeter*
a heart condition	**o boală de inimă**
	oh bwaler deh eeneemer
high/low blood pressure	**tensiunea prea mare/prea mică.** *tensee-ooneh-a preh-a mareh/preh-a meecer*
I'm on...	**Iau...** *Ya°°*

For What to Take, see page 158.

Treatment

Do I need a prescription/medicine?	**Am nevoie de o rețetă/un medicament?** *am nevoyeh deh oh retseter/oon medeecament*
Can you prescribe a generic drug [unbranded medication]?	**Puteți prescrie un medicament generic?** *pootetsy prescree-eh oon medeecament jenereec*
Where can I get it?	**De unde îl pot lua?** *deh oondeh eel pot looa*

YOU MAY HEAR...

Care este problema? *careh yesteh problema*
What's wrong?
Unde vă doare? *oondeh ver dwareh*
Where does it hurt?
Vă doare aici? *ver dwareh a-eechy*
Does it hurt here?
Urmați vreun tratament?
oormatsy vreh-oon tratament
Are you on medication?
Sunteți alergic la ceva?
soontetsy alergeec la cheva
Are you allergic to anything?
Deschideți gura. *descheedetsy goora*
Open your mouth.
Respirați adînc. *resperatsy aduhnc*
Breathe deeply.
Tușiți, vă rog. *tuscheetsy ver rog*
Cough, please.
Mergeți la spital. *mergetsy la speetal*
Go to the hospital.

Hospital

Notify my family, please.	**Vă rog anunțați-mi familia.** *ver rog anoontsatsy-my fameelee-a*
I'm in pain.	**Am dureri.** *am doorery*
I need a doctor/nurse.	**E nevoie de un doctor/o asistentă.** *yeh nevoyeh deh oon doctor / o aseestenter*
When are visiting hours?	**Care sunt orele de vizită?** *careh soont oreleh deh veezeeter*
I'm visiting...	**Îmi vizitez...** *uhmy veezeetez...*

Dentist

I have...		
	a broken tooth	**Am un dinte spart.** *am oon deenteh spart*
	a lost filling	**Mi-a căzut o plombă.** *mya cerzoot o plomber*

a toothache	**Mă doare dintele/măseaua.** *mer dwareh deenteleh/*
	mersawa
Can you fix this denture?	**Puteţi să-mi reparaţi proteza?**
	pootetsy sermy reparatsy proteza

Gynecologist

I have cramps/ a vaginal infection.	**Am o infecţie vaginală.**
	am o eenfectsee-eh vajeenaler
I missed my period.	**Nu mi-a venit ciclul.** *noo mee-ah veneet cheeclool*
I'm on the Pill.	**Iau anticoncepţionale.**
	yaoo anteeconcheptsee-onaleh
I'm (...months) pregnant.	**Sunt gravidă (în luna...).**
	soont graveeder (....uhn loona)
I'm not pregnant.	**Nu sunt gravidă.** *noo soont graveeder*
My last period was...	**Ultima dată mi-a venit ciclul pe...**
	oolteema dater mee-a veneet cheeclool peh...

For Numbers, see page 166.

Optician

I lost...	**Mi-am pierdut...** *my-am pyerdoot...*
a contact lens	**o lentilă de contact** *o lenteeler deh contact*
my glasses	**ochelarii** *ochelaree*
a lens	**o lentilă** *o lenteeler*

Payment & Insurance

How much?	**Cât costă?** *cuht coster*
Can I pay by credit card?	**Pot plăti cu această carte de credit?**
	pot plertee coo achaster carteh deh credeet
I have insurance.	**Am asigurare.** *am aseegoorareh*
I need a receipt for my insurance.	**Am nevoie de o chitanţă pentru asigurarea mea.**
	am nevoyeh deh o keetantser pentroo aseegoorareh-a meh-a

Pharmacy

ESSENTIAL

Where's the pharmacy?	**Unde se află o farmacie (non stop) prin apropiere?** _oondeh seh afler o farmachee-eh preen preen apropee-ereh_
What time does it open/close?	**La ce oră se deschide/închide farmacia?** _la cheh orer seh deskeedeh/uhnkeedeh farmachee-a_
What would you recommend for...?	**Ce îmi recomandați pentru...?** _cheh uhmy recomandatsy pentroo..._
How much do I take?	**Câte trebuie să iau?** _cuhteh trebooyeh ser yaoo_
I'm allergic to...	**Sunt alergic m/alergică f...** _soont alerjeec/ alerjeecer_

What to Take

How much do I take?	**Câte trebuie să iau?** _cuhteh trebooyeh ser yaoo_
How often?	**Cât de des?** _cuht deh des_
Is it safe for children?	**Nu este periculos pentru copii?** _noo yesteh pereecoolos pentroo copeey_
I'm taking...	**Iau...** _yaoo_
Are there side effects?	**Există efecte secundare?** _egzeester efecteh secoondareh_
I need something for...	**Am nevoie de ceva pentru...** _am nevoyeh deh cevah pentroo..._
a cold	**răceală** _rerchaler_
a cough	**tuse** _tooseh_
diarrhea	**diaree** _dee-are-eh_
a headache	**durere de cap** _doorereh deh cap_
insect bites	**întepături de insecte** _uhntsepertoory deh eensecteh_

motion sickness	**rău de mișcare** _rer^{oo}deh meesh<u>ca</u>reh_
a sore throat	**o durere în gât** _o doorereh uhn guht_
sunburn	**arsuri de soare** _ar<u>soor</u>y deh s<u>wa</u>reh_
a toothache	**o durere de dinți** _o doorereh deh <u>deen</u>ts^y_
an upset stomach	**stomac deranjat** _sto<u>mac</u> deran<u>zh</u>at_

Basic Supplies

I'd like…	**Dați-mi** _datsee-mee_
acetaminophen [paracetamol]	**acetaminofen** _acetameenopfen_
antiseptic cream	**o cremă antiseptică** _o <u>cre</u>mer antee<u>sep</u>teecer_
aspirin	**niște aspirină** _<u>neesh</u>teh aspee<u>ree</u>ner_
bandages	**un bandaj** _oon ban<u>da</u>zh_
a comb	**un pieptene** _oon <u>pyep</u>terneh_
condoms	**niște prezervative** _<u>neesh</u>teh prezerva<u>teeveh</u>_
contact lens solution	**lichid pentru lentile de contact** _lee<u>keed</u> <u>pen</u>troo len<u>tee</u>leh deh con<u>tact</u>_
deodorant	**un deodorant** _oon deodo<u>rant</u>_
a hairbrush	**o perie de păr** _o <u>pe</u>ree-eh deh perr_
hairspray	**un fixativ de păr** _oon feexa<u>teev</u> deh perr_
ibuprofen	**ibuprofen** _eebooprofen_
insect repellent	**un spray contra insectelor** _oon spray <u>con</u>tra een<u>sec</u>telor_
lotion	**loțiune** _lotyooneh_
a nail file	**o pilă de unghii** _o <u>pee</u>ler deh <u>oon</u>gee_
a (disposable) razor	**un aparat de ras** _oon apar<u>at</u> deh ras_
razor blades	**niște lame** _<u>neesh</u>teh <u>la</u>meh_
sanitary napkins [pads]	**niște tampoane externe** _<u>neesh</u>teh tamp<u>wa</u>neh ex<u>ter</u>neh_
shampoo	**un șampon** _oon sham<u>pon</u>_

conditioner	**balsam de păr** *balsam deh per*
soap	**un săpun** *oon serpoon*
sunscreen	**cremă de protecţie solară**
	cremer deh protectsee-eh solarer
tampons	**nişte tampoane interne**
	neeshteh tampwaneh eenterneh
tissues	**nişte batiste de hârtie**
	neeshteh bateesteh deh huhrtee-eh
toilet paper	**nişte hârtie igienică**
	neeshteh huhrtee-eh eejee-eneecer
toothpaste	**o pastă de dinţi** *o paster deh deentsy*

For Baby Essentials, see page 145.

YOU MAY SEE...

de ... ori pe zi	once/three times a day
tabletă	tablet
picătură	drop
linguriţă	teaspoon
...mese	...meals
după	after
înainte	before
cu	with
pe stomacul gol	on an empty stomach
a se înghiţi întregi	swallow whole
poate cauza somnolenţă	may cause drowsiness
a nu se înghiţi	do not ingest

The Basics

Grammar : Regular Verbs

There are five main conjugations of verbs which are distinguished by the ending of the infinitive: **-a, -ea, -e, -i** and **-î.**

	a învăța (to learn)	a vedea (to see)	a face (to make, do)	a vorbi (to speak)
eu	învăț	văd	fac	vorbesc
tu	înveți	vezi	faci	vorbești
el/ea	învață	vede	face	vorbește
noi	învățăm	vedem	facem	vorbim
voi	învățați	vedeți	faceți	vorbiți
ei/ele	învață	văd	fac	vorbesc

Irregular Verbs

Here are three common irregular verbs:

	a fi (to be)	a avea (to have)	a lua (to take)
eu	sunt	am	iau
tu	ești	ai	iei
el/ea	este	are	ia
noi	suntem	avem	luăm
voi	sunteți	aveți	luați
ei/ele	sunt	au	iau

Note: Verbs often appear in Romanian without a personal pronoun because the ending of the verb is sufficient to indicate the subject. Personal pronouns precede the verb only for emphasis

The **perfect tense** is formed with the help of the auxilliary verb **a avea** "to have" followed by the past participle of the verb used.
Verbs with infinitives ending in **-a, -i** and **-î** form the past participle by adding **-t**; those with an **-ea** ending replace it with **-ut**; others ending in **-e** replace it with either **-ut** or **-s**:

infinitive		past participle	
a invita	invitat	am invitat	I (have) invited
a vedea	văzut	a văzut	he/she/it say (has seen)
a face	făcut	ați făcut	you did (have done)
a se duce	dus	s-au dus	they went (have gone)

The **future tense** is formed in two main ways:

1. by using the colloquial **o să** plus the subjunctive (similar to the present tense in all forms except the third person).

O să stau o lună	I'll be staying a month.
O să venim la ora opt.	We'll come at eight.

2. by using the auxiliary forms **voi, vei, va, vom, veți** and **vor** placed in front of the infinitive form of the verb without **a**.

eu voi pleca I shall leave	**noi vom pleca** we shall leave
tu vei pleca you shall leave	**voi veți pleca** you shall leave
el/ea va pleca he/she shall leave	**ei/ele vor pleca** they shall leave

Negations

The negative is formed by putting the negation **nu** in front of the verb; eg:

eu nu locuiesc aici	I do not live here
eu nu am locuit aici	I did not live here
eu nu voi locui aici	I will not live here

With the verb a avea "to have", the negative is often reduced to **n-**:

n-am I don't have	**n-aveți** you don't have

Nouns & Articles

In Romanian, nouns belong to three genders: masculine, feminine and neuter. Nouns ending in a consonant are usually masculine or neuter, and nouns that end in a vowel are generally feminine. Although there are many exceptions in the plural form, masculine nouns usually end in -**i**; feminine nouns end in -**i**, and neuter nouns end in -**e** or -**uri**.

pom – pomi	tree – trees (masc.)
excursie – excursii	trip – trips (fem.)
scaun – scaune	chair – chairs (neut.)

1. Indefinite article (a)

The indefinite article is **un** for masculine nouns, **o** for feminine nouns and **un** for neuter nouns. With plural forms, the invariable article **nişte** "some" is used.

(masc.)	**un călător** a traveler	**nişte călători** some travelers
(fem.)	**o piesă** a play	**nişte piese** some plays
	o librărie a bookshop	**nişte librării** some bookshops
	o carte a book	**nişte cărţi** some books
(neut.)	**un spectacol** a show	**nişte spectacole** some shows
	un taxi a taxi	**nişte taxiuri** some taxis

2. Definite article (the)

In Romanian, there is no separate word for the definite article; instead a particle is placed at the end of the noun, depending on its gender and number; the definite articles for singular nouns are **ul, -a, -ul,** and for plural **are -i,** and **-le**.

(masc.)	**copac** tree	**copacul** the tree	**copacii** the trees
(fem.)	**casă** house	**casa** the house	**casele** the houses
(neut.)	**hotel** hotel	**hotelul** the hotel	**hotelurile** the hotels
	birou office	**biroul** the office	**birourile** the offices

Adjectives

The **adjective** agrees in number, case and gender with the **noun** it describes. It usually follows the noun but certain common adjectives precede the noun. The table that follows shows the declension of **nouns, adjectives** and **indefinite articles**.

	masc.	fem.	neut.
	a good doctor	a good map	a good hotel
SINGULAR			
subject **direct object**	un doctor bun	o hartă bună	un hotel bun
poss. object **indirect object**	unui doctor bun	unei hărți bune	unui hotel bun
PLURAL			
subject **direct object**	niște doctori buni	niște hărți bune	niște hoteluri bune
possessive object	unor doctori buni	unor hărți bune	unor hoteluri bune

Note the different forms of the possessive object (**of...or...'s**) and the indirect object (**to...**). Each case is illustrated in the examples below:

Un doctor bun este foarte ocupat.	A good doctor is very busy.
Puteți să chemați un doctor bun?	Can you get me a good doctor?
Biroul unui doctor bun est curat.	A good doctor's office is clean.
El a împrumutat cartea lui unui doctor bun.	He lent his book to a good doctor.

Demonstrative adjectives

	masc.	fem.	neut.
this	**acest(a)**	**această (aceasta)**	**acest(a)**
these	**acești(a)**	**aceste(a)**	**aceste(a)**
that	**acel(a)**	**acea/aceea**	**acel(a)**
those	**acei(a)**	**acele(a)**	**acele(a)**

These adjectives can be placed either before or, for particular emphasis, after the noun. When placed after the noun, they take the endings of the definte article form (shown in brackets).

Possessive Adjectives

	singular			plural		
	masc.	fem.	neut.	masc.	fem	neut.
pronoun particle	**al**	**a**	**al**	ai	**ale**	**ale**
my	**meu**	**mea**	**meu**	mei	**mele**	**mele**
your	**tău**	**ta**	**tău**	tăi	tale	tale
his/her/its	**său**	**lui/sa/ei**	**lui/ei/său**	săi/lui/ei	**lui/sale/ei**	**sale**
our	**nostru**	**noastră**	**nostru**	noștri	**noastre**	**noastre**
your	**vostru**	**voastră**	**vostru**	voștri	**voastre**	**voastre**

Invariable adjectives are used for "their" – **lor**, and the formal form of "you" – **dumneavoastră**. When they are not the subject of the sentence, **ei** "her" and **lui** "his" replace the forms of **său**.

The possessive pronoun is formed by preceding the possessive adjective with the pronoun particle.

e.g. **pâinea noastră** our bread   **cărţile sunt ale mele** the books are mine

Personal pronouns

	Subject	Direct Object	Indirect Object	Reflexive
I	**eu**	**mă**	**îmi**	**mă**
you (sing.)	**tu**	**te**	**îţi**	**te**
he, it	**el**	**îl**	**îi**	**se**
she	**ea**	**o**	**îi**	**se**
we	**noi**	**ne**	**ne**	**ne**
you (plur.)	**voi/** dumneavoastră	**vă**	**vă**	**vă**
they (masc.)	**ei**	**îi**	**le**	**se**
they (fem.)	**ele**	**le**	**le**	**se**

Romanian has four forms for the word "you".

tu for addressing a close friend or child (singular)

dumneata (d-ta) for addressing a colleague (singular)

voi for addressing close friends (plural)

dumneavoastră (dvs.) for addressing one or more strangers or people older than yourself; this is the most respectful term and should be used when in doubt.

Numbers

ESSENTIAL

0	**zero**	*zero*
1	**unu**	*oonoo*
2	**doi**	*doy*
3	**trei**	*tray*
4	**patru**	*patroo*
5	**cinci**	*cheenchy*
6	**şase**	*shaseh*
7	**şapte**	*shapteh*
8	**opt**	*opt*
9	**nouă**	*no-wer*
10	**zece**	*zecheh*
11	**unsprezece**	*oonsprezecheh*
12	**doisprezece**	*doysprezecheh*
13	**treisprezece**	*traysprezecheh*
14	**paisprezece**	*pighsprezecheh*
15	**cincisprezece**	*cheenchysprezecheh*
16	**şaisprezece**	*shighsprezecheh*
17	**şaptesprezece**	*shaptesprezecheh*
18	**optsprecece**	*optsprezecheh*
19	**nouăsprezece**	*no-wersprezecheh*

20	**douăzeci** *do-werzechy*
21	**douăzeci și unu** *do-werzechy shee oonoo*
22	**douăzeci și doi** *do-werzechy shee doy*
30	**treizeci** *trayzechy*
31	**treizeci și unu** *trayzechy shee oonoo*
40	**patruzeci** *patroo*
50	**cincizeci** *cheenchyzechy*
60	**șaizeci** *shighzechy*
70	**șaptezeci** *shaptehzechy*
80	**optzeci** *optzechy*
90	**nouăzeci** *no-werzechy*
100	**o sută** *o sooter*
101	**o sută unu** *o sooter oonoo*
200	**două sute** *do-wer sooteh*
500	**cinci sute** *cheenchy sooteh*
1,000	**o mie** *o mee-eh*
10,000	**zece mii** *zecheh mee*
1,000,000	**un milion** *oon meelee-on*

Ordinal Numbers

first	**primul (prima)** *preemool (preema)*
second	**al doilea (a doua)** *al do-eeleh-a (a do-wa)*
third	**al treilea (a treia)** *al tre-eeleh-a (a tre-ya)*
fourth	**al patrulea (a patra)** *al patrooleh-a (a patra)*
fifth	**al cincilea (a cincea)** *al cheencheeleh-a (a cheencheh-a)*
once	**o dată** *o dater*
twice	**de două ori** *deh do-wer ory*
three times	**de trei ori** *deh tray ory*

Time

ESSENTIAL

What time is it?	**Cât e ora?** *cuht ye ohrah*
It's midday.	**Este amiază.** *yesteh ameeaser*
At midnight.	**la miezul nopţii** *la myezool noptsee*
From one o'clock to two o'clock.	**De la ora unu la ora două.** *deh la ohrah oonoo la ora do-wer*
Five past three.	**Trei şi cinci.** *trey shee cheenchy*
A quarter to ten.	**Zece fără un sfert.** *zecheh fer-rer oon sfehrt*
5:30 a.m./p.m.	

Days

ESSENTIAL

Monday	**luni** *loony*
Tuesday	**marţi** *martsy*
Wednesday	**miercuri** *myercoory*
Thursday	**joi** *zhoy*
Friday	**vineri** *veenery*
Saturday	**sâmbătă** <u>suhmb</u>erter
Sunday	**duminică** *doo<u>mee</u>neecer*

Dates

yesterday	**ieri** *yery*
today	**azi** *azy*
tomorrow	**mâine** *muhyneh*
day	**zi** *zee*

week	**săptămână** *serptermuhner*
month	**lună** *looner*
year	**an** *an*

Months

January	**ianuarie** *yanoo-aree-eh*
February	**februarie** *febroo-aree-eh*
March	**martie** *martee-eh*
April	**aprilie** *apreelee-eh*
May	**mai** *migh*
June	**iunie** *yoonee-eh*
July	**iulie** *yoolee-eh*
August	**august** *aoogoost*
September	**septembrie** *septembree-eh*
October	**octombire** *octombree-eh*
November	**noiembrie** *noyembree-eh*
December	**decembrie** *dechembree-eh*

Seasons

spring	**primăvară** *preemervarer*
summer	**vară** *varer*
autumn	**toamnă** *twamner*
winter	**iarnă** *yarner*

Holidays

January 1/ New Year's Day	**Întâi Ianuarie/Anul Nou** *uhntuhy yanoo-aree-eh anool noᵒᵒ*
May 1/Labor Day	**Întâi Mai** *uhntuhy migh*
All Saints Day/Nov 1	**Luminaţia** *lumeenatseea*
December 25	**Crăciun** *crerchoon*
Moveable Feasts	
Good Friday	**Vinerea Mare** *veenereh-a Mareh*

Easter	**Paşte** _pashteh_
Easter Monday	**Lunea Paştilor** _looneh-a Pashteelor_
Ascension	**Înălţarea** _uhnerltsareh-a_
Pentecost	**Rusaliile** _roosaleeleh_

Conversion Tables

When you know	Multiply by	To find
ounces	28.3	grams
pounds	0.45	kilograms
inches	2.54	centimeters
feet	0.3	meters
miles	1.61	kilometers
square inches	6.45	sq. centimeters
square feet	0.09	sq. meters
square miles	2.59	sq. kilometers
pints (U.S./Brit)	0.47/0.56	liters
gallons (U.S./Brit)	3.8/4.5	liters
Fahrenheit	5/9, after 32	Centigrade
Centigrade	9/5, then+32	Fahrenheit

Mileage

1 km – 0.62 mi	20 km – 12.4 mi
5 km – 3.10 mi	50 km – 31.0 mi
10 km – 6.20 mi	100 km – 61.0 mi

Measurement

1 gram	gram khrahm	= 0.035 oz.
1 kilogram (kg)	kilogram kee·loa·khrahm	= 2.2 lb
1 liter (l)	liter lee·tuhr	= 1.06 U.S./0.88 Brit. quarts
1 centimeter (cm)	centimeter sehn·tee· may·tuhr	= 0.4 inch
1 meter (m)	meter may·tuhr	= 3.28 feet
1 kilometer (km)	kilometer kee·loa·may·tuhr	= 0.62 mile

Temperature

-40° C	–	-40° F
-30° C	–	-22° F
-20° C	–	-4° F
-10° C	–	14° F
-5° C	–	23° F
-1° C	–	30° F
0° C	–	32° F
5° C	–	41° F
10° C –	–	50° F
15° C	–	59° F
20° C	–	68° F
25° C	–	77° F
30° C	–	86° F
35° C	–	95° F

Oven Temperature

100° C	–	212° F	177° C	–	350° F
121° C	–	250° F	204° C	–	400° F
149° C	–	300° F	260° C	–	500° F

Dictionary

A

abbey mănăstire *f*
abbreviation abreviere *nt*
about (approximately) vreo, cam
above deasupra
abscess abces *nt*
absent nu-i aici
absorbent cotton vată *f*
accept, to a accepta
accessories accesorii *nplt*
accident accident *nt*
account cont *nt* bancar
ache durere *f*
adaptor adaptor *nt*
address adresă *f*
address book agendă f de adrese
adhesive colant
adhesive tape scoci *nt*
admission intrare *f*
admitted admis
Africa Africa *f*
after după
after-shave lotion lotiune f după ras
afternoon, in the după-amiaza *f*
again din *nou*
age vârstă *f*
ago (two years) în urmă cu; acum (doi ani)
air bed saltea f pneumatică
air conditioning aer *nt* conditionat
air mattress saltea f pneumatică
airmail par avion
airplane avion *nt*
airport aeroport *nt*
aisle seat loc *nt* la culoar
alarm clock radio-ceas *nt*
alcohol alcool *nt*
alcoholic alcoolic
all tot
allergic alergic
almond migdală *f*
alphabet alfabet *nt*
also de asemenea

alter, to (garment) a modifica
altitude sickness rău nt de altitudine
amazing uluitor
amber chihlimbar *nt*
ambulance salvare *f*
American american *m*
American plan pensiune f completă
amethyst ametist *nt*
amount sumă *f*
amplifier amplificator *nt*
anaesthetic anestetic *nt*
analgesic calmant *nt*
and și
animal animal *nt*
aniseed anason *nt*
ankle genunchi *m*
anorak hanorac *nt*
another altul *m*; alta *f*
answer răspuns *nt*
antibiotic antibiotic *nt*
antidepressant antidepresiv *nt*
antique shop magazin *nt* de antichități
antiques antichități *fpl*
antiseptic cream cremă f antiseptică
any nici un
anyone cineva
anything ceva; nimic
anywhere pe undeva
apartment apartament *nt*
aperitif aperitiv *nt*
appendicitis apendicită *f*
appendix apendice *nt*
appetizer antreu *nt*
apple măr *nt*
appliance aparatură *f*
appointment programare *f*; întâlnire *f*
apricot caisă *f*
April aprilie *m*
archaeology arheologie *f*
architect arhitect *m*
area code prefix *nt*
arm brat *nt*

| **adj** adjective | **BE** British English | **prep** preposition |
| **adv** adverb | **n** noun | **v** verb |

around (approximately) jur de
arrangement (set price) tarif nt
arrival sosiri fpl
arrive, to a ajunge; a veni; a sosi
art artă f
art gallery galerie f de artă
artichoke anghinare f
article obiect nt
artificial artificial
artificial light lumină f artificială
artist artist m
ashtray scrumieră f
Asia Asia
ask for, to a spune; a comanda
asparagus sparanghel m
aspirin aspirină f
asthma astmă f
astringent lotiune f astringentă
at la
at least cel putin
at once imediat
aubergine vânătă f
August august m
aunt mătuşă f
Australia Australia
Austria Austria
automatic automat nt
autumn toamnă f
average in medie
awful groaznic; urât

B

baby copil m
babysitter îngrijitoare f de copii, babysitter f
back spate nt
back, to be/to get a se întoarce
backache durere f de spate
backpack rucsac nt
bacon şuncă f
bacon and eggs şuncă şi ouă
bad rău
bag sac m; pungă f
baggage bagaj nt
baggage cart cărucior nt de bagaje
baggage check birou nt de bagaje; înregistrarea f bagajelor
baggage locker cabină f de bagaje; birou nt de bagaje
baked copt

baker's brutărie f
balance (finance) balanţă f
balcony balcon nt
ball-point pen pix nt cu pastă
ball (inflated) minge f
ballet balet nt
banana banană f
Band-Aid® pansamente ntpl
bandage bandaj nt
bangle brăţară f
bangs breton nt
bank (finance) bancă f
banknote bancnotă f
bar (room) bar nt
barber's frizer m
basil busuioc nt
basketball baschet nt
bath baie f
bath salts săruri de baie fpl
bath towel prosop nt de baie
bathing cap cască f de înot
bathing hut cabină f de schimb
bathing suit costum nt de baie
bathrobe halat nt de baie
bathroom baie f
battery baterie f
be, to a fi
beach plajă f
beach ball minge f de plajă
bean fasole f
beard barbă f
beautiful frumos
beauty salon salon nt de cosmetică
bed pat nt
bed and breakfast cazare şi micul dejun
bedpan oală f de noapte
beef vacă f
beer bere f
beet(root) sfeclă f roşie
before (time) înainte
beginner începător m
beginning început nt
behind înapoi; în spate
beige bej
Belgium Belgia
bell (electric) sonerie f
Belorus Bielorusia f
below dedesubt
belt curea f

bend (road) curbă f
berth cuşetă de dormit f
better mai bine
between între
bicycle bicicletă f
big mare
bilberry afină f
bill nota f de plată; (banknote) bancnotă f
billion (Am.) bilion nt
binoculars binoclu nt
bird pasăre f
birth naştere f
birthday zi f de naştere
biscuit (Br.) biscuit nt
bitter amar
black negru
black and white (film) alb-negru
black coffee cafea f neagră (turcească)
blackberry mură f
blackcurrant coacăz nt negru
bladder vezică f urinară
blade lamă f
blanket pătură f
bleach decolorant nt
bleed, to a sângera
blind (window shade) jaluzea f
blister băşică f
blocked înfundat
blood sânge nt
blood pressure tensiune f arterială; puls nt
blood transfusion transfuzie f de sânge
blouse bluză f
blow-dry un pieptănat nt
blue albastru
blueberry afină f
blusher ruj nt de obraz
boat barcă f
bobby pin agrafă f
body corp nt
boil uruncul m
boiled fiert
boiled egg ou fiert nt
bone os nt
book carte f
booking office agenţie f de voiaj
booklet (of tickets) carnet nt de bilete
bookshop librărie f
boot cizmă f
born născut

botanical gardens grădină f botanică
botany botanică f
bottle sticlă f
bottle-opener deschizător nt de sticle
bottom jos nt
bow tie papion nt
bowel intestin nt
box cutie f
boxing box nt
boy băiat m
boyfriend prieten m
bra sutien nt
bracelet brăţară f
braces (suspenders) bretele fpl
braised fiert înăbuşit
brake frână f
brake fluid lichid nt de frână
brandy ţuică f
bread pâine f
break, to a sparge; a rupe
break down, to a avea o pană de motor
breakdown pană f
breakdown van maşină f de depanare
breakfast micul dejun nt
breast sân m
breathe, to a respira
bridge pod nt
bring down, to a aduce
bring, to a aduce
British britanic m
broken defect; spart, rupt
brooch broşă f
brother frate m
brown maro
bruise vânătaie f
Brussels sprouts varză f de Bruxelles
bubble bath spumă f de baie
bucket găleată f
buckle cataramă f
build, to a construi
building clădire f
building blocks/bricks cuburi ntpl
bulb (light) bec nt
Bulgaria Bulgaria f
bump (lump) umflătură f
burn arsură f
burn out, to (bulb) a se arde
bus autobuz nt
bus stop staţie f de autobuz

business afaceri *fpl*
business class clasa *f* business
business district zona *f* băncilor
business trip scop *nt* de serviciu
busy ocupat
but dar
butane gas gaz *nt* butan; butelie *f* de gaz
butcher's măcelărie *f*
butter unt *nt*
button nasture *m*
buy, to a cumpăra

C

cabana cabană *f*
cabbage varză *f*
cabin (ship) cabină *f*
cable legătură *f*
cable car teleferic *nt*
cable release declanşator *nt*
café cafe-bar *nt*
cake prăjitură *f*
calculator calculator *nt*
calendar calendar *nt*
call (phone) apel *nt* telefonic
call, to (give name) a se zice; (phone) a telefona
call, to (summon) a da; a chema
call back, to a suna înapoi
calm liniştit
cambric batist *nt*
camel-hair păr *nt* de cămilă
camera aparat *nt* de filmat; aparat de fotografiat
camera case port-aparat *nt*
camera shop magazin *nt* de aparate foto
camp site camping *nt*; loc *nt* de campare
camp, to a campa
campbed pat de camping *nt*
camping camping *nt*
camping equipment echipament *nt* de camping
can opener deschizător *n* de conserve *t*
can (be able to) a putea să
can (container) cutie *f* de conservă
Canada Canada *f*
Canadian canadian *m*
cancel, to a anula
candle lumânare *f*
candy dropsuri *ntpl*

cap şapcă *f*
capers capere *fpl*
capital (finance) capital *nt*
car maşină *f*
car hire închirieri *fpl* auto
car mechanic mecanic *m* auto
car park parcare *f*
car racing raliu *nt*
car radio radio *nt* de maşină
car rental agenţie *f* de închiriat maşini
carafe carafă *f*
carat carat *nt*
caravan rulotă *f*
caraway chimen *m*
carbon paper hârtie *f* indigou
carbonated (fizzy) apă *f* gazoasă
carburettor carburator *nt*
card carte *f* de joc *f*; carte *f* de visita
card game joc de cărţi *nt*
cardigan jachetă *f*
carp crap *m*
carpet carpetă *f*
carrot morcov *m*
cart cărucior *nt*
carton (of cigarettes) cartuş *nt* de ţigări; pachet *nt* de ţigări
cartridge (camera) încărcător *nt* de film
case port-aparat *nt*
cash desk casă *f*
cash, to a încasa
cassette casetă *f*
cassette recorder casetofon *nt*
castle castel *nt*
catalogue catalog *nt*
cathedral catedrală *f*
Catholic catolic
cauliflower conopidă *f*
caution atenţie *f*
cave peşteră *f*
celery ţelină *f*
cemetery cimitir *nt*
centimetre centimetru *m*
centre centru *nt*
century secol *nt*
ceramics ceramică *f*
cereal cereală *f*
certain sigur
certificate certificat *nt*
chain (jewellery) lănţişor *nt*

chain bracelet brătară f lănțișor
chair scaun nt
chamber music muzică f de cameră
change, to a schimba; bani ntpl mărunti
chapel capelă f
charcoal cărbune nt pentru grătar
charge cost nt; tarif nt; taxă f
charge, to a plăti; a reține
charm bracelet brătară f cu talismanuri
charm (trinket) talisman nt
cheap ieftin
check (Am.) cec nt
check (restaurant) nota f de plată
check, to a verifica; a controla; (luggage) a înregistra
check-up (medical) examen nt medical
check in, to (airport) a înregistra bagajele
check out, to a pleca, a părăsi
cheers! noroc nt
cheese brânză f
chemist's farmacie f
cheque cec nt
cherry cireșe fpl
chess șah nt
chess set joc nt de șah
chest piept nt
chestnut castană f
chewing gum gumă f de mestecat
chewing tobacco tutun nt de mestecat
chicken pui m
chicken breast piept nt de găină
chicory andive fpl
chiffon șifon nt
child copil m
children's doctor doctor pediatru m
China China f
chips cartofi mpl prăjiti
chives arpagic nt
chocolate ciocolată f
chocolate bar baton nt de ciocolată
chop (meat) cotlet nt
Christmas Crăciun nt
chromium crom nt
church biserică f
cigar trabuc nt
cigarette țigară f
cigarette case tabacheră f
cigarette holder port-țigaret nt
cigarette lighter brichetă f

cine camera cameră f de filmat
cinema cinema nt
cinnamon scorțișoară f
circle (theatre) balcon nt
city oraș nt
city centre centrul nt orașului
classical clasic
clean curat
clean, to a spăla
cleansing cream lapte demachiant nt
cliff stâncă f
clip clamă f
cloakroom garderoba f
clock ceas nt
clock-radio radio-ceas nt
close, to a închide
clothes haine fpl
clothes peg/pin cârlig nt de rufe
clothing îmbrăcăminte f
cloud nor m
clove cuișoare fpl
coach (bus) autocar nt
coat haină f
coconut nucă f de cocos
coffee cafea f
coins numismatica f
cold rece; frig
cold (illness) răceală f; gripă f
cold cuts salamuri npl
collar guler nt
collect call convorbire f cu taxă inversă
colour culoare f; color
colour chart paletă f de culori
colour rinse șampon nt colorant
colour shampoo șampon nt colorant
colour slide diapozitiv nt color
colourfast nu iese la spălat
comb pieptene m
comedy comedie f
commission (fee) comision nt
common (frequent) curent
compact disc compact disc nt
compartment (train) loc nt
compass busolă f
complaint reclamație f
concert concert nt
concert hall sală de concert f
condom preservativ m
conductor (orchestra) dirijor m

conference room sală f de conferințe
confirm, to a confirma
confirmation confirmare f
congratulation felicitări fpl
connection (transport) legătura f de tren
constipation constipație f
consulate consulat nt
contact lens lentile fpl de contact
contagious contagios
contain, to a conține
contraceptives anticoncepționale ntpl
contract contract nt
control control nt
convent mănăstire f
cookie fursec n
cool box geantă f frigorifică
copper cupru nt
coral coral m
corduroy velur nt
corkscrew tirbușon nt
corn plaster leucoplast nt pentru bătături
corn (sweet) porumb nt
corn (foot) bătătură f
corner colt nt
cost pret nt; cost nt
cost, to a costa
cot pătut nt
cotton bumbac nt
cotton wool vată f
cough tuse f
cough drops picături fpl de tuse
cough, to a tuși
counter ghișeu nt
country țară f
countryside la tară
courgette dovlecel m
court house tribunal nt
cousin văr m
crab crab m
cramp cârcel m
crayfish (river) rac m
crayon creion nt
cream frișcă f
cream (toiletry) cremă f
crease resistant nu se șifonează
credit credit nt
credit card carte f de credit
crepe crep

crisps cartofi mpl cipși
crockery veselă f
cross cruce f
crossing (maritime) traversare f
crossroads intersecție f
cruise croazieră f
crystal cristal nt
cucumber castravete m
cuff link buton nt de manșetă
cuisine mâncăruri fpl
cup ceașcă f
curler bigudiu nt
currants stafide fpl
currency schimb nt
currency exchange office birou n de schimb
current urent nt de apă
curtain perdea f
curve (road) curbă f
customs vamă f
cut (wound) tăietură f
cut, to (with scissors) a tunde
cut off, to (interrupt) a întrerupe
cut glass sticlă f șlefuită
cutlery tacâmuri ntpl
cutlet cotlet nt
cycling ciclism nt
cystitis cistită f
Czech Republic Republica Cehă f

D

dairy magazin nt de brânzeturi și lactate
dance dans nt
dance, to a dansa
danger pericol nt
dangerous periculos
dark întuneric; închis
date (appointment) întâlnire f
date (day) dată f
date (fruit) curmale fpl
daughter fată f
day zi f
day off zi liberă f
daylight lumină f de zi
decade deceniu nt
decaffeinated decofeinizat
December decembrie m
decision decizie f
deck chair șezlong nt
deck (ship) punte f

declare, to (customs) a declara
deep adânc
degree (temperature) grad nt
delay întârziere f
delicatessen magazin nt de delicatese
deliver, to a livra
delivery livrare f
denim doc nt
Denmark Danemarca f
dentist dentist m
denture proteză f
deodorant deodorant nt
department store magazin universal nt
department (museum) departament nt;
(shop) raion nt
departure plecări fpl
deposit (down payment) depunere f; avans nt
dessert desert nt
detour (traffic) deviere f
develop, to a developa
diabetic diabetic
dialling code prefix nt telefonic
diamond diamant nt
diaper [nappy] scutec nt de unică folosinţă
diarrhoea diaree f
dictionary dicţionar nt
diesel motorină f
diet regim n alimentar
difficult greu
difficulty dificultate f
digital ceas nt digital
dill mărar nt
dining car vagon restaurant nt
dining room sufragerie f; sala de mese f
dinner (have) a cină f; a lua masa de seară
direct direct
direct, to a îndruma
direction direcţie f
director (theatre) regizor m
directory (phone) anuar nt
disabled persoană invalidă fpl
disc disc nt
discotheque discotecă f
discount reducere f
disease boală f
dish mâncare f
dishwashing detergent detergent nt de vase
disinfectant desinfectant nt

dislocated dislocat
dissatisfied nemultumit
disturb, to a deranja
diversion (traffic) deviere f
dizzy ametit
do, to a face
doctor doctor m
doctor's office cabinet nt medical
dog câine m
doll păpuşă f
dollar dolar m
double bed pat nt dublu
double room cameră f de două persoane
down jos
downtown centru nt
dozen duzină f
drawing paper hârtie f de desenat
drawing pins pioneze fpl
dress rochie f
dressing gown capot nt
drink băutură f
drink, to a bea
drinking water apă f potabilă
drip, to a curge
drive, to a conduce
driving licence carnet nt de conducere
drop (liquid) picătură f
drugstore farmacie f
dry uscat; sec
dry cleaner's curăţătorie f
dry shampoo şampon nt
duck raţă f
dummy (baby's) suzetă f
during în timpul
duty (customs) vamă f
dye vopsea f

E

each fiecare
ear ureche f
earache durere f de urechi
early devreme
earring cercel m
east est nt
Easter Paşte m
easy uşor
eat, to a mânca
eel ţipar m
egg ou nt

eggplant vânătă f
eight opt
eighteen optsprezece
eighth al optulea
eighty optzeci
elastic bandage bandaj nt elastic
electrical appliance aparatură f electrică
electrical goods shop magazin nt de aparate electrice
electricity electricitate f
electric(al) electric(e)
electronic electronic
elevator lift nt
eleven unsprezece
embarkation point punct nt de îmbarcare
embassy ambasadă f
embroidered brodat
embroidery broderie f
emerald smarald nt
emergency urgenţă f
emergency exit ieşire f de incendiu
emery board pilă f
empty gol
enamel email nt
end sfârşit nt
engaged (phone) ocupat
engagement ring inel nt de logodnă
engine (car) motor nt
England Anglia f
English englez; englezesc
enjoy oneself, to a se distra
enjoyable minunat
enlarge, to a mări
enough destul
entrance intrare f
entrance fee intrare f
envelope plic nt
equipment echipament nt
eraser gumă f
escalator escalator nt; lift nt
estimate (cost) cost nt aproximativ; preţ nt estimativ
Eurocheque eurocec nt
Europe Europa f
evening seară f
evening dress ţinută obligatorie f; (woman's) rochie de seară f
evening, in the seara
everything tot, toate

exchange, to a schimba
exchange rate curs nt de schimb
excursion excursie f
excuse me pardon
exercise book caiet nt
exhaust pipe ţeavă f de eşapament
exhibition expoziţie f
exit ieşire f
expect, to a aştepta
expenses cheltuieli fpl
expensive scump
exposure (photography) expunere f
exposure counter dispozitiv nt de numărătoare
express expres (tren) nt
expression expresie f
expressway autostradă f
extension (phone) interior nt
extension cord/lead prelungitor nt
extra în plus
eye ochi m
eye drops picături fpl de ochi
eye shadow fard nt de pleope
eye specialist medic m oculist
eyebrow pencil creion nt de sprâncene
eyesight vedere f

F

fabric (cloth) pânzeturi fpl
face faţă f
face pack mască f
face powder pudră f de obraz
factory uzina f
fair târg nt
fall (autumn) toamnă f
fall, to a cădea
family familie f
fan belt curea f de ventilator
far departe
fare (ticket) costul nt (biletului)
farm fermă f
fast rapid (tren) nt
fat (meat) gras
father tată m
faucet robinet nt
fax fax nt
February februarie m
fee (doctor's) plată f
feeding bottle biberon nt

feel, to (physical state) a simți
felt fetru *nt*
felt-tip pen carioca *nt*
ferry bac *nt*
fever febra *f*
few puțini; (a few) câțiva
field câmp *nt*
fifteen cincisprezece
fifth al cincilea
fifty cincizeci
fig smochina *f*
file (tool) pila *f*
fill in, to a completa
filling (tooth) plomba *f*
filling station stație *f* de benzina
film film *nt*
film winder maneta *f* de rulat filmul
filter filtru *nt*
filter-tipped cu filtru
find, to a gasi
fine (OK) bine
fine arts arte *fpl* frumoase
finger deget *nt*
Finland Finlanda *f*
fire foc *nt*
first primul
first-aid kit trusa *f* de prim ajutor
first class clasa *f* întâi
first name prenume *nt*
fish pește *m*
fishing a pescui
fishing tackle unelte *ntpl* de pescuit
fishmonger's pescarie *f*
fit, to a proba
fitting room cabina *f* de proba
five cinci
fix, to a trata
fizzy (mineral water) (apa minerala) gazoasa *f*
flannel flanela *f*
flash (photography) blitz *nt*
flash attachment legatura *f* de blitz
flashlight lanterna *f*
flat (apartment) apartament *nt*
flat (shoe) pantofi *mpl* plati (fara toc)
flat tyre roata *f* dezumflata
flea market talcioc *nt*
flight zbor *nt*
floor palier *nt*

floor show spectacol *nt* în mijlocul publicului
florist's florarie *f*
flour faina *f*
flower floare *f*
flu gripa *f*
fluid lichid *nt*
foam rubber mattress saltea *f* de burete de cauciuc
fog ceata *f*
folding chair scaun *nt* pliant
folding table masa *f* plianta
folk music muzica *f* populara
follow, to a urma
food mâncare *f*
food poisoning intoxicatie *f* alimentara
foot laba *f* piciorului, picior *nt*
foot cream crema *f* de picioare
football fotbal *n*
footpath poteca *f*
for pentru
forbidden interzis
forecast prevedere *f*
forest padure *f*
forget, to a uita
fork furculita *f*
form (document) formular *nt*
fortnight doua saptamâni
fortress cetate *f*
forty patruzeci
foundation cosmetic fond de ten *nt*
fountain fântâna *f*
fountain pen stilou *nt* cu cerneala
four patru
fourteen paisprezece
fourth al patrulea
fowl pasare *f*
frame (glasses) rama *f*
France Franța *f*
free liber; gratuit
French bean fasole *f* fideluța
Friday vineri *f*
fried prajit
fried egg ou *nt* prajit
friend prieten *m*
fringe breton *nt*
from de la
frost ger *nt*
fruit fruct *nt*
fruit cocktail cocteil *nt* de fructe

fruit juice suc nt de fructe
fruit salad salată f de fructe
frying pan tigaie f
full plin
full board pensiune f completă
full insurance asigurare f casco
furniture mobilă f stil
furrier's blănărie f

G

gabardine gabardină f
gallery galerie f de artă
game joc nt
game (food) vânat
garage garaj nt; servis nt
garden grădină f
gardens grădina f publică
garlic usturoi m
gas gaz nt
gasoline benzină f
gastritis gastrită f
gauze tifon nt
gem piatră f prețioasă
general uzuale; general
general delivery post restant nt
general practitioner doctor m de medicină
    generală; generalist m
genitals organe genitale ntpl
gentlemen bărbați mpl
geology geologie f
Germany Germania f
get, to (find) a lua
get off, to a coborî
get past, to a face loc
get to, to a ajunge
get up, to a se da jos din pat
gherkin castravete m murat
gift cadou nt
gin gin nt
gin and tonic gin cu apă tonică
ginger ghimber m
girdle centură f
girl fată f
girlfriend prietenă f
give, to a da; a pune
give way, to (traffic) a ceda (trecerea)
gland glandă f
glass pahar nt
glasses ochelari npl

gloomy sumbru
glove mănușă f
glue lipici nt
go, to a merge
go away! pleacă de aici
go back, to a se întoarce
go out, to a ieși
gold aur nt
gold plated aurit
golden auriu
golf golf nt
golf course teren nt de golf
good bun
good afternoon bună ziua
good-bye la revedere
good evening bună seara
good morning bună dimineata
good night noapte bună
goose gâscă f
gooseberries agrișe fpl
gram(me) gram nt
grammar gramatică f
grammar book carte f de gramatică
grapes struguri mpl
grapefruit grepfrut nt
grapefruit juice suc nt de grepfrut
gray gri
graze julitură f
greasy (păr) gras
Great Britain Marea Britanie f
Greece Grecia f
green verde
green bean fasole verde f
greengrocer's aprozar nt
greeting salut nt
grey gri
grilled grătar nt
grocery (grocer's) băcănie f
groundsheet folie f de mușama
group grup nt
guesthouse hotel-pensiune nt
guide ghid nt
guidebook ghid nt
guinea fowl bibilică f
gum (teeth) gingie f
gynaecologist ginecolog m

H

hair păr nt

hair dryer uscător *nt* de păr
hair gel gel *nt* de păr
hair lotion loțiune *f* de păr
hair spray fixativ *nt* de păr
hairbrush perie *f* de păr
haircut tunsoare *f*
hairdresser coafor *nt*
hairgrip clamă *f*
hairpin ac de păr *nt*
half jumătate *f*
half an hour jumătate *f* de oră
half board demipensiune *f*
half price jumătate *f* de pret
hall porter valet *m*
ham șuncă *f*
ham and eggs șuncă și ouă
hammer ciocan *nt*
hammock hamac *nt*
hand mână *f*
hand cream cremă *f* de mâini
hand washable de spălat de mână
handbag geantă *f*; poșeta *f*
handicrafts artizanat *nt*
handkerchief batistă *f*
handmade lucrat de mână
hanger umeraș *nt*
happy fericit
harbour port *nt*
hard dur
hard-boiled (egg) ou *n* (fiert) tare
hare iepure *m*
hat pălărie *f*
have, to a avea
have to, to (must) a trebui, a fi necesar
hay fever alergie *f* la polen
hazelnut alune *fpl* de pădure
he el
head cap *nt*
head waiter ospătar *m* șef
headache durere de cap *f*
headphones căști *fpl*
health insurance form formular *nt* de asigurare
heart inimă *f*
heart attack atac *nt* de cord
heat, to a încălzi
heavy greu; puternic
heel toc *nt*
height înălțime *f*

helicopter helicopter *nt*
hello bună; (telephone) alo
help! ajutor
help, to a ajuta
her a ei
herb tea ceai *nt* de plante medicinale
herbs mirodenii *fpl*
here aici
hi bună
high înălțime *f*; mare
high season în sezon
hill deal *nt*
hire închiriere *f*
hire, to a închiria
his a lui
history istorie *f*
hitchhike, to a face autostop
hold on! (phone) așteptați
hole gaură *f*
holiday vacantă *f*
holidays vacantă; concediu *nt*
home casă *f*
home address adresa *f* de acasă
home town orașul *nt*
honey miere *f*
hope, to a spera
horse racing curse fpl de cai
horseback riding călărie *f*
hospital spital *nt*
hot water apă *f* caldă
hot-water bottle buiotă *f* cu apă fierbinte
hot cald; (boiling) fierbinte
hotel hotel *nt*
hotel directory/guide ghid *nt* al hotelurilor
hotel reservation rezervare *f* la hotel
hour oră *f*
house casă *f*
household article articol *nt* de uz casnic
how far cât de departe
how long cât timp
how many câti *mpl*, câte *fpl*
how much cât
hundred o sută
hungry foame *f*
hunting vânătoare *f*
hurry, to be in a a se grăbi
hurt (to be) (a fi) rănit
hurt, to a durea
husband soț *m*

hydrofoil navă *f* cu aripi portante

I

I eu
ice gheață *f*
ice cream înghețată *f*
ice cube cuburi *ntpl* de gheață
ice pack pungă *f* cu cuburi de gheață
iced tea ceai *nt* rece
icon icoană *f*
if dacă
ill bolnav *m*, bolnavă *f*
illness boală *f*
important important
imported importat
impressive impresionant
in în
include, to a include
included inclus
India India *f*
indigestion indigestie *f*
inexpensive nu prea scump
infected infectat
infection infecție *f*
inflammation inflamație *f*
inflation inflație *f*
inflation rate rata *f* inflației
influenza gripă *f*
information informație *f*
injection injecție *f*
injure, to a (se) răni
injured rănit
injury rană *f*
ink cerneală *f*
inquiry informație *f*
insect bite înțepătură *f* de insectă
insect repellent spray *nt* contra insectelor
insect spray insecticid *nt*
inside înăuntru
instrument (musical) instrument *nt* muzical
insurance asigurare *f*
insurance company companie *f* de asigurări
interest (finance) dobândă *f*
interested, to be a fi interesat
interesting interesant
international international
interpreter interpret *m*
intersection intersecție *f*
introduce, to a prezenta

introduction (social) prezentare *f*
investment investiție *f*
invitation invitație *f*
invite, to a invita
invoice factură *f*
iodine iod *nt*
Ireland Irlanda *f*
Irish irlandez *m*
iron (for laundry) fier *nt* de călcat
iron, to a călca
ironmonger's fierărie *f*
it acest
Italy Italia *f*
its al său, a sa, ai săi, ale sale
ivory fildeș *nt*

J

jacket jachetă *f*
jade jad *nt*
jam (preserves) gem *nt*
jam, to a se bloca
January ianuarie *m*
Japan Japonia *f*
jar (container) borcan *nt*
jaundice icter *nt*
jaw maxilar *nt*
jazz jazz *nt*
jeans blugi *mpl*
jersey jerseu *nt*
jewel box cutie *f* de bijuterii
jeweller's magazin *nt* de bijuterii; bijuterie *f*
joint încheietură *f*
journey călătorie *f*
juice suc *nt*
July iulie *m*
jumper pulover *nt*
June iunie *m*
just (only) doar

K

keep, to a tine
kerosene gaz *nt*
key cheie *f*
kidney rinichi *mpl*
kilo(gram) kilogram *nt*
kilometre kilometru *m*
kind amabil
kind (type) fel *nt*
knee genunchi *m*

kneesocks șosete lungi *fpl*
knife cuțit *nt*
knock, to a ciocăni
know, to a ști

L

label etichetă *f*
lace dantelă *f*
ladies femei *fpl*
lake lac *nt*
lamb (meat) miel *m*
lamp lampă *f*
landscape peisaj *nt*
language limbă *f*
lantern felinar *nt*
large mare
last ultimul; trecut
last name numele *nt* de familie
late târziu
late, to be a rămâne în urmă
laugh, to a râde
launderette spălătorie *f* Nufărul
laundry service servicii *ntpl* de spălătorie
laundry (clothes) rufe *fpl* de spălat
laundry (place) spălătorie *f*
laxative laxativ *nt*
lead (metal) plumb *nt*
lead (theatre) rol *nt* principal
leap year an bisect *m*
leather piele *f*
leave, to a pleca; (deposit) a lăsa
leeks praz *nt*
left stânga
left-luggage office birou *nt* de bagaje
leg picior *nt*
lemon lămâie *f*
lemonade limonadă *f*
lens (camera) obiectiv *nt*
lens (glasses) lentilă *f*
lentils linte *f*
less mai puțin
lesson lecție *f*
let, to (hire out) a închiria
letter scrisoare *f*
letter box cutie *f* poștală
letter of credit scrisoare *f* acreditivă
lettuce salată *f* verde
library bibliotecă *f*
licence (driving) carnet *nt* de conducere

lie down, to a se întinde
life belt colac *nt* de salvare
life boat barcă *f* de salvare
life guard (beach) salvamar *m*
lift (elevator) lift *nt*
light ușor; (colour) deschis
light (lamp) lumină *f*
light (for cigarette) foc *nt*
light meter celulă *f* fotoelectrică
lighter brichetă *f*
lighter fluid/gas gaz *nt* de brichetă
lightning fulger *nt*
like ca
like, to a vrea; (please) a plăcea
linen (cloth) in *nt*
lip buză *f*
lipsalve strugurel *nt* de buze
lipstick ruj *nt* de buze
liqueur lichior *nt*
listen, to a asculta
litre litru *nt*
little (a little) puțin
live, to a locui
liver ficat *m*
lobster homar *m*
local local *nt*
long lung
long-sighted prezbit *m*
look, to a se uita
look for, to a căuta
look out! atenție
loose (clothes) largi
lose, to a pierde
loss pierdere *f*
lost rătăcit
lost and found/lost property office birou *nt* de obiecte pierdute
lot (a lot) mult
lotion loțiune *f*
loud (voice) (cu voce) tare
lovely frumos
low mic
low season în afara sezonului
lower de jos
luck noroc *nt*
luggage bagaj *nt*
luggage locker cabină de bagaje *f*; birou *nt* de bagaje

luggage trolley cărucior *nt* de bagaje
lump (bump) umflătură *f*
lunch dejun *nt*; masa *f*
lung plămân *nt*

M

machine (washable) (care se spală la) mașina
mackerel macrou *n*
magazine revistă *f*
magnificent magnific
maid cameristă *f*
mail poșta *f*
mail, to a pune la poștă
mailbox cutie *f* de scrisori
main important; principal
make, to a face
make up, to (prepare) a face
make-up machiaj *nt*
make-up remover pad tampon *nt* pentru demachiat
mallet ciocan *nt*
man bărbat *m*; om *m*
manager director *m*
manicure manichiură *f*
many multi *m*, multe *f*
map hartă *f*
March martie *m*
marinated marinat(ă)
marjoram măghiran *nt*
market piață *f*
marmalade marmeladă *f*
married căsătorit
mass (church) slujbă *f* religioasă
matt (finish) mat
match (matchstick) chibrit *nt*,
match (sport) meci *nt*
match, to (colour) a potrivi
material (cloth) material *nt*
matinée matineu *nt*
mattress saltea *f*
May mai *m*
may (can) a permite
meadow pajiște *f*
meal masă *f*
mean, to a însemna
means miljoace *npl*
measles pojar *nt*
measure, to a măsura

meat carne *f*
meatball chiftele *fpl*
mechanic mecanic *m*
mechanical pencil creion *nt* mecanic
medical certificate certificat *nt* medical
medicine medicină *f*; (drug) medicament *nt*
medium-sized de capacitate medie
medium (meat) bine făcut, potrivit
meet, to a întâlni
melon pepene *m* galben
memorial monument *nt* comemorativ
mend, to a repara
menthol (cigarettes) tigări *fpl* mentolate
menu meniu *nt*
merry fericit
message masaj *nt*
metre metru *m*
mezzanine (theatre) balcon *nt*
middle mijloc
midnight miezul noptii *nt*
mild (light) slab
mileage kilometraj *nt*
milk lapte *nt*
milliard miliard *nt*
million milion *nt*
mineral water apă *f* minerală
minister (religion) pastor *m*
mint mentă *f*
minute minut *nt*
mirror oglindă *f*
miscellaneous diverse
Miss domnișoară *f*
miss, to a lipsi
mistake greșeală *f*
moccasin mocasini *mpl*
modified American plan demipensiune *f*
moisturizing cream cremă *f* hidratantă
moment moment *nt*
monastery mănăstire *f*
Monday luni
money bani *mpl*
money order mandat *nt*
month lună *f*
monument monument *nt*
moon lună *f*
moped motoretă *m*
more mai mult
morning, in the dimineata

mortgage ipotecă f
mosque moschee f
mosquito net plasă f contra tăntarilor
motel motel nt
mother mamă f
motorbike motocicletă f
motorboat barcă f cu motor
motorway autostradă f
mountain munte m
mountaineering alpinism nt
moustache mustață f
mouth gură f
mouthwash apă f de gură
move, to a mişca
movie film m
movie camera cameră f de filmat
movies filme ntpl
Mr. domnul m
Mrs. doamna f
much mult
mug cană f
muscle muşchi m
museum muzeu nt
mushroom ciupercă f
music muzică f
musical comedie f muzicală
must (have to) a trebui; avea nevoie; a crede
mustard muştar nt
my al meu

N

nail (human) unghie f
nail brush periuță f de unghii
nail clippers foarfece nt de unghii cu arc
nail file pilă f de unghii
nail polish ojă f de unghii
nail polish remover acetonă f
nail scissors foarfece nt de unghii
name nume nt
napkin şervetel nt
nappy scutec nt
narrow strâmt
nationality naționalitate f
natural natural
natural history ştiințele fpl naturale
nausea greață f
near aproape; lângă
nearby în apropiere
nearest cel mai aproape

neat (drink) (băutură) f simplă
neck gât nt
necklace colier nt
need, to a avea nevoie de
needle ac nt
negative negativ nt
nephew nepot m
nerve nerv m
Netherlands Olanda f
never niciodată
new nou
New Year Anul Nou m
New Zealand Noua Zeelandă f
newsagent's chioşc nt de ziare
newspaper ziar nt
newsstand chioşc nt de ziare
next următorul; viitor
next to lângă
nice (beautiful) frumos
niece nepoată f
night noapte f
night, at la noapte
night cream cremă f de noapte
nightclub club nt de noapte
nightdress/-gown pijama f
nine nouă
nineteen nouăsprezece
ninety nouăzeci
ninth al nouălea
no nu
noisy zgomotos
nonalcoholic nealcoolic
none niciunul m; niciuna f
nonsmoker nefumător m
noodles tăiței mpl
noon la amiază f
normal normal
north nord nt
North America America de Nord f
Norway Norvegia f
nose nas nt
nose drops picături de nas fpl
nosebleed a curge sânge din nas
not nu
note paper hârtie f de scris
note (banknote) bancnotă f
notebook carnet nt
nothing nimic

notice (sign) anunţ *nt*
notify, to a înştiinţa
November noiembrie *m*
now acum
number număr *nt*
nurse soră (medicală) *f*
nutmeg nucşoară *f*

O

o'clock oră *f*
occupation (profession) ocupaţia *f*
occupied ocupat
October octombrie *m*
office birou *nt*
oil ulei *nt*
oily (greasy) gras
old vechi, bătrân
old town -olive măslin *m*
on pe
on foot pe jos
on request staţie *f* facultativă
on time la timp
once o dată
one unu
one-way (traffic) sens unic *nt*
one-way ticket un (bilet) dus *nt*
onion ceapă *f*
only numai; doar
onyx onix *nt*
open deschis
open, to a deschide
open-air în are liber
opera operă *f*
opera house operă *f*
operation operaţie *f*
operator centrala *f*
opposite vis-a-vis
optician optician *m*
or sau
orange (fruit) portocală *f*
orange (colour) portocaliu
orange juice suc *nt* de portocale
orchestra orchestră *f*
orchestra (seats) stal *nt*
order (goods, meal) comandă *f*
order, to (goods, meal) a comanda
oregano sovârv *m*
ornithology ornitologie *f*
other alt

our al nostru
out of order deranjat; nu funcţionează
out of stock stoc *nt* terminat
outlet (electric) priză *f*
outside afară
oval oval
overalls salopete *fpl*
overdone (meat) prea prăjită
overheat, to (engine) a încălzi peste măsur
overtake, to a depăşi
owe, to a datora

P

pacifier (baby's) suzetă *f*
packet pachet *nt*
pail găletică *f*
pain durere *f*
painkiller calmant *nt*
paint vopsea *f*
paint, to a picta
paintbox cutie *f* de culori
painter pictor *m*
painting pictură *f*; tablou *nt*
pair pereche *f*
pajamas pijama *f*
palace palat *nt*
palpitations palpitaţii *fpl*
panties chiloţi *mpl*
pants (trousers) pantaloni *mpl*
panty girdle burtieră *f*
panty hose ciorapi *mpl* cu chilot
paper hârtie *f*
paper napkin şerveţel *nt* de hârtie
paperback carte *f*
paperclip agrafă *f* pentru hârtie
paraffin (fuel) parafină *f*
parcel colet *nt*
pardon, I beg your poftim/poftiţi
parents părinţi *mpl*
park parc *nt*
park, to a parca
parking parcare *f*
parking lot parcare *f*
parliament building clădirea *f* parlamentulu
parsley pătrunjel *m*
partridge potârniche *f*
party (social gathering) petrecere *f*
pass (mountain) trecătoare *f*
pass, to (driving) a trece

ass through, to a trece
assport pașaport nt
assport photo fotografie f de pașaport
asta paste făinoase fpl
aste (glue) clei nt
astry shop plăcintărie f
atch, to (clothes) a pune un petec
ath potecă f
atient pacient m
attern model nt
ay, to a plăti
ayment plată f
ea mazăre f
each piersică f
eak vârf nt
eanut arahidă f
ear pară f
earl perlă f
edestrian pieton m
eg (tent) cârlig nt de cort
en stilou nt
encil creion nt
encil sharpener ascuțitoare f
endant pandantiv m
enicillin penicilină f
enknife briceag m
ensioner pensionar m
eople oameni mpl
epper piper m
er cent procent nt
er day pe zi
er hour pe oră
er night pe noapte
er person de persoană
er week pe săptămână
ercentage procentaj nt
erch biban m
erform, to (theater) a juca
erfume parfum nt
erhaps poate
eriod pains dureri fpl la ciclu
eriod (monthly) ciclu nt
ermanent wave permanent nt
ermit permis nt
erson persoană f
ersonal personal
ersonal call/person-to-person call a da un telefon
ersonal cheque cec nt personal

petrol benzină f
pewter aliaj nt cu cositor
pharmacy farmacie f
pheasant fazan m
photo poză f; fotografie f
photocopy fotocopie f
photographer atelier nt de fotografiat
photography fotografie f
phrase frază f
pick up, to (person) a lua
picnic picnic nt
picnic basket coș nt de picnic
picture (painting) tablou nt
picture (photo) poză f
pig porc m
pigeon porumbel m
pike știucă f
pill somnifer nt
pillow pernă f
pin ac nt; agrafă f
pineapple ananas m
pink roz
pipe pipă f
pipe cleaner instrument nt pentru curătat pipa
pipe tobacco tutun nt de pipă
pipe tool dispozitiv *nt* de curătat pipă
place, to a da
place loc nt
place of birth locul nt nașterii
plain (colour) simplă
plane avion nt
planetarium planetar m
plaster gips nt
plastic plastic
plastic bag pungă f de plastic
plate farfurie f
platform (station) peron nt
platinum platină f
play (theatre) piesă f
play, to a cânta; a juca
playground teren nt de joc
playing card cărți fpl de joc,
please vă rog
plimsolls teniși mpl
plug (electric) ștecher nt
plum prună f
pneumonia pneumonie f
poached fiert în apă

pocket buzunar nt
pocket calculator calculator nt de buzunar
pocket watch ceas nt de buzunar
point of interest (sight) obiectiv nt turistic important
point, to a arăta
poison otravă f
poisoning intoxicaţie f (alimentară)
pole (ski) prăjină f
pole (tent) stâlp m de cort
police poliţie f
police station post nt de poliţie; centru nt de poliţie
pond iaz nt
poplin poplin nt
pork porc m
port port nt
portable portabil
porter hamal m; portar m
portion porţie f
Portugal Portugalia f
possible, (as soon as) (cât de curând) posibil
post office poşta f
post (mail) poşta f
post, to a pune la poştă
postage costul nt prin poştă
postage stamp timbru nt
postcard vedere f
poste restante post restant nt
potato cartof m
pottery olărit nt
poultry păsări fpl
pound liră f sterlină
powder pudră f
powder compact pudră f compactă
powder puff puf nt de pudră
pregnant gravidă f
premium (gasoline) benzină f super
prescribe, to a prescrie
prescription reţetă f
present cadou nt
press stud capsă f
press, to (iron) a călca
pressure presiune f; tensiune f
pretty drăguţ
price preţ nt; cost nt; tarif nt
priest preot m
print (photo) poză f

private particular
processing (photo) developat
profession (occupation) ocupaţie f
profit profit nt
programme program nt
pronounce, to a pronunţa
pronunciation pronunţie f
propelling pencil creion nt mecanic
Protestant protestant m
provide, to a puna la dispoziţie
prune prune fpl uscate
public holiday sărbătoare f legală
pull, to (tooth) a trage; a extrage
pullover pulovăr nt
pump pompă f
puncture (flat tyre) pană f de cauciuc
purchase achiziţie f
pure pur
purple roşu-închis, purpuriu
push, to a împinge
put, to a pune
pyjamas pijama f

Q
quail prepeliţă f
quality calitate f
quantity cantitate f
quarter sfert nt
quarter of an hour sfert nt de oră
quartz cuart nt
question întrebare f
quick(ly) repede
quiet linişte f

R
rabbi rabin m
rabbit iepure m
race course/track hipodrom nt
racket (sport) rachetă f
radiator (car) radiator nt
radio radio nt
radish ridiche f
railway cale ferată f
railway station gară f
rain ploaie f
rain, to a ploua
raincoat haină f de ploaie
raisin stafidă f
rangefinder telemetru nt

rare (meat) crudă; în sânge
rash egzemă f
raspberry zmeură f
rate (inflation) rată f
rate (price) cost nt
razor aparat nt de ras
razor blades lamă f de ras
reading lamp lampă f de citit
ready gata
real (genuine) veritabil
rear coada f
receipt chitanţă f
reception recepţie f
receptionist recepţionist m
recommend, to a recomanda
record (disc) disc nt
record player pick-up nt
rectangular rectangular(ă)
red roşu; **wine** vin nt roşu
reduction reduce f
refill (pen) rezervă f de stilou
refund (to get a) (a primi) banii mpl înapoi
regards salutări fpl
register, to (luggage) a înregistra
registered mail (scrisoare) f recomandată f
registration înregistrare f
registration form formular nt de înregistrare
regular (petrol) (benzină) f normală
religion religie f
religious service slujbă f religioasă
rent, to a închiria
rental închiriere f
repair a repara
repair, to a repara
repeat, to a repeta
report, to (a theft) a raporta
request staţie f facultativă
required cerut
reservation rezervaţie f
reservations office birou nt de rezervări
reserve, to a rezerva
reserved rezervat
rest rest nt
restaurant restaurant nt
return, to (come back) a se întoarce; (give back) a înapoia
return ticket bilet nt dus-întors
rheumatism reumatism nt

rib coastă f
ribbon panglică f
rice orez nt
right (correct) bine
right (direction) dreapta
ring (jewellery) inel nt
ring, to (doorbell) a suna
river râu nt
river trip croazieră f
road drum nt
road assistance asistenţă f rutieră
road map harta f drumurilor
road sign semn nt de circulaţie
roast beef friptură f de vacă
roasted prăjit
roll chiflă f
roll-neck pulover nt cu guler pe gât
roll film bobină f de film
roller skate patine fpl cu rotile
Romania România f
Romanian (language) româneşte
room cameră f
room number numărul nt camerei
room service serviciu nt de cameră
room (space) spaţiu nt
rope frânghie f
rosary rozariu nt
rosemary rozmarin m
rouge ruj nt
round rotund
round-neck pulover nt cu guler în jurul gâtului
round-trip ticket bilet nt dus-întors
round up, to a rotunji
route traseu nt
rowing boat barcă f cu rame
rubber (eraser) gumă f
rubber (material) cauciuc nt
ruby rubin nt
rucksack rucsac nt
ruin ruină f
ruler (for measuring) linie f
rum rom nt
running water apă f curentă
Russia Rusia f

S

safe seif n
safe (free from danger) nu este periculos
safety pin ac nt de siguranţă

saffron șofran m
sage salvie f
sailing navigatie f
sailing boat barcă f cu pânze
salad salată f
sale (bargains) solduri ntpl; (commerce) vânzare f
salt sare f
salty sărat
same acelaşi
sand nisip nt
sandals sandale fpl
sandwich sendvici nt; sandviş nt
sanitary napkin/towel tampon nt extern
sapphire safir nt
sardines sardele fpl
satin satin nt
Saturday sâmbătă f
sauce sos nt
saucepan cratiță f
saucer farfurioară f
sauerkraut varză f acră
sausage cârnati mpl
scarf fular nt
scarlet roșu-aprins; stacojiu
scenery peisaj nt
scenic route traseu nt turistic (spre)
scissors foarfece nt; foarfecă f
scooter scuter nt
Scotland Scotia f
scrambled eggs scrob nt
screwdriver șurubelniță f
sculptor sculptor m
sculpture sculptură f
sea mare f
seafood fructe ntpl de mare
season anotimp nt
seasoning condimente ntpl
seat loc nt
second al doilea; secundă f
second class clasa f a doua
second-hand shop consignatie f
second hand (watch) secundar nt
secretary secretară f
section raion nt
see, to a vedea; a întâlni
self-service shop magazin nt cu autoservire
sell, to a vinde
send, to a trimete; a livra; a expedia

sentence propozitie f
separately separat
September septembrie m
seriously grav
service serviciu nt
service (church) slujbă f religioasă
serviette șervetel nt
set menu meniu nt fix
set (hair) bigudiuri ntpl
setting lotion fixativ nt
seven șapte
seventeen șaptesprezece
seventh al șaptelea
seventy șaptezeci
sew, to a coase
shade (colour) culoare f
shampoo șampon nt
shampoo and set șampon și bigudiuri
shape măsură f
share (finance) actiune f
sharp (pain) (durere) acută
shave ras nt
shaver aparat nt de ras
shaving brush pămătuf nt de ras
shaving cream cremă f de ras
she ea
shelf raft nt
ship vapor nt
shirt cămaşă f
shivery frisoane npl
shoe pantof m
shoe polish cremă f de pantofi
shoe shop magazin nt de încaltaminte
shoelace șiret nt de pantofi
shoemaker's cizmar m
shop magazin nt
shop window vitrină f
shopping area centru nt comercial
shopping centre centru nt comercial
short scurt
short-sighted miop
shorts șort nt
shoulder umăr m
shovel lopătică f
show spectacol nt
show, to a arăta
shower duș nt
shrimp crevete m
shrink, to a intra la apă

hut închis
shutter (window) oblon nt; **(camera)** obturator nt
sick (ill) bolnav m
sickness (illness) boală f
side parte f
sideboards/-burns perciuni mpl
sightseeing excursie f
sightseeing tour traseu nt
signs (notice) semne ntpl
sign, to a semna
signet ring inel nt cu sigiliu
silk mătase f
silver argint nt; **(colour)** argintiu
silver plated argintat
silverware argintărie f
simple simplu
since de, din
sing, to a cânta
single cabin cabină f pentru o persoană
single room cameră f cu un pat
single (ticket) un dus
single (unmarried) necăsătorit
sister soră f
sit down, to a sta jos
six șase
sixteen șaisprezece
sixth al șaselea
sixty șaizeci
size mărime f
size (clothes, shoes) măsură f
skate patină f
skating rink patinoar nt
ski schi nt
ski, to a schia
ski boot ghete fpl de schi
ski lift teleschi nt
ski run pistă f
skiing schi nt
skiing equipment echipament nt de schi
skiing lessons lectii fpl de schi
skin piele f
skin-diving a plonja
skin-diving equipment echipament nt de plonjat
skirt fustă f
sky cer nt
sleep, to a dormi

sleeping bag sac nt de dormit
sleeping car vagon nt de dormit
sleeping pill somnifer nt
sleeve mânecă f
sleeveless fără mânecă
slice felie f
slide (photo) diapozitiv nt
slip (underwear) jupon nt
slipper papuc m
Slovakia Slovacia f
slow down, to a reduce viteza
slow(ly) mai putin repede; mai încet; mai rar
small mic
smoke, to a fuma
smoked afumat
smoker fumător m
snack gustare f
snack bar chioșc nt cu gustări
snap fastener capsă f
sneaker pantofi mpl de tenis
snorkel tub nt de scafandru
snow zăpadă f
snuff tutun nt de prizat
soap săpun nt
soccer fotbal nt
sock șosetă f
socket (electric) priză f
soft-boiled (egg) (ou) moale
soft drink băutură f răcoritoare
soft (lens) lentile fpl flexibile
sole (shoe) talpă f
soloist solist m
some niște
someone cineva
something ceva
somewhere undeva
son băiat m
song cântec nt
soon curând
sore throat durere f de gât
sore (painful) dureros
sorry scuzati; regret
sort (kind) fel nt
soup supă f
south sud nt
South Africa Africa de Sud f
South America America de Sud
souvenir suvenir nt

souvenir shop magazin nt de suveniruri
spade lopăţică f
Spain Spania f
spare tyre roată f de rezervă
sparkling (wine) (vin) spumos nt
spark(ing) plug bujie f
speak, to a vorbi
speaker (loudspeaker) difuzor nt
special special
special delivery de urgenţa
specialist specialist m
speciality specialitate f
specimen (medical) recoltare f
spectacle case port-ochelari nt
speed viteză f
spell, to a se scrie
spend, to a cheltui
spice condiment nt
spinach spanac nt
spine coloană f vertebrală
sponge burete m
spoon lingură f
sport sport nt
sporting goods shop magazin nt cu articole
    de sport
sprained luxat
spring (season) primăvară f
spring (water) izvor nt
square pătrat nt; (town) piaţă f
stadium stadion nt
staff (personnel) personal nt
stain pată f
stalls (theatre) stal nt
stamp (postage) timbru nt
staple capsă f
star stea f
start, to a începe
starter (meal) antreu nt
station (railway) gară f
station (underground, subway) staţie f de
    metrou; (metrou) nt
stationer's papetărie f
statue statuie f
stay sejur nt
stay, to a sta; (reside) a locui
steal, to a fura
steamed în aburi
stew tocană f

stewed fiert
stiff neck durere f de ceafă
still (mineral water) (apă) simplă f
sting înţepătură f
sting, to a înţepa
stitch, to a coase
stock exchange bursă f
stocking ciorap m
stomach stomac nt
stomach ache durere f de burtă
stools scaun nt
stop (bus) staţie f de autobuz
stop, to a opri; a sta
stop! opreşte!
stop thief! hoţii!
store (shop) magazin nt
straight ahead drept înainte
straight (drink) băutură f simplă
strange straniu
strawberry căpşună f
street stradă f
street map harta f străzilor; harta oraşului
streetcar tramvai nt
string sfoară f
strong tare; puternic
student student m
study, to a studia
stuffed umplut
sturdy durabilă
sturgeon sturion m
subway (railway) metrou nt
suede piele f de căprioară
sugar zahăr nt
suit (man's) costum nt bărbătesc; (woman's)
    costum nt de damă
suitcase valiză f
summer vară f
sun soare m
sun-tan cream cremă f de bronzat
sun-tan oil ulei nt de bronzat
sunburn arsură f de soare
Sunday duminică f
sunglasses ochelari ntpl de soare
sunstroke insolaţie f
super (petrol) super
superb superb
supermarket magazin nt alimentar
suppository supozitoare ntpl

surgery (consulting room) cabinet nt medical
surname numele nt de familie
suspenders (Am.) bretele fpl
swallow, to a înghiți
sweater pulover nt
sweatshirt bluză f de trening din bumbac
Sweden Suedia f
sweet dulce
sweet corn porumb m
sweet shop magazin nt de dulciuri
sweet (confectionery) dulciuri ntpl
sweetener zaharină f
swell, to a (se) umfla
swelling umflătură f
swim, to a înota
swimming înot nt
swimming pool piscină f
swimming trunks costum nt de baie
swimsuit costum nt de înot
switch (electric) buton nt, întrerupător nt
switchboard operator telefonist(ă) m/f
Switzerland Elveția f
swollen umflat
synagogue sinagogă f
synthetic sintetic
system sistem nt

T

T-shirt cămașă f
table masă f
tablet (medical) tabletă f
tailor's croitor m
take, to a lua; a merge; (time) a dura
take away, to de luat acasă
taken (occupied) liber
talcum powder pudră f de talc
tampon tampon nt intern
tangerine mandarină f
tap (water) (apă de la) robinet nt
tape recorder casetofon nt
tapestry tapiserie f
tarragon tarhon m
tart tartă f
tax taxă f; TVA
taxi taxi nt
taxi rank/stand stație f de taxi
tea ceai nt
team echipă f

teaspoon linguriță f
telegram telegramă f
telegraph office birou PTT nt
telephone telefon nt
telephone, to (call) a telefona
telephone booth telefon nt
telephone call apel nt telefonic
telephone directory anuar nt telefonic
telephone number număr nt de telefon
telephoto lens teleobiectiv nt
television televizor nt
telex telex nt
telex, to a trimete un telex
tell, to a spune
temperature temperatură f
temporary provizoriu
ten zece
tendon tendon nt
tennis tenis nt
tennis court teren nt de tenis
tennis racket rachetă f de tenis
tent cort nt
tent peg cârlig nt de cort
tent pole stâlp m de cort
tenth al zecelea
term (word) termen m
terrace terasă f
terrifying îngrozitor
tetanus tetanus nt
than decât
thank you mulțumesc
thank, to a mulțumi
that acela
theatre teatru nt
theft furt nt
their al lor
then atunci
there acolo
thermometer termometru nt
these aceștia mpl; acestea fpl
they ei mpl; ele fpl
thief hot m
thigh coapsă f
thin subtire
think, to (believe) a crede
third al treilea
thirsty, to be a îți fi sete
thirteen treisprezece

thirty treizeci
this asta; acesta
those acelea
thousand o mie f
thread ață f
three trei
throat gât nt
throat lozenge pastile fpl pentru dureri de gât
through prin
through train tren nt direct
thumb degetul nt mare
thumbtack pioneză f
thunder tunet nt
thunderstorm furtună f
Thursday joi f
thyme cimbru m
ticket bilet nt
ticket office casă f de bilete
tie cravată f
tie clip clamă f de cravată
tie pin ac nt de cravată
tight (close-fitting) strâmt
tights dresuri ntpl
time oră f
time (occasion) oră f; zi f
timetable (trains) mersul nt trenurilor
tin (container) cutie f de conserve
tin opener deschizător nt de conserve
tint vopsea f
tinted fumuriu
tire (tyre) roată f
tired obosit
tissue (handkerchief) batistă de hârtie f
to până la
to get (fetch) a comanda
to get (go) a ajunge
to get (obtain) a obține; a cumpăra
toast pâine f prăjită
tobacco tutun nt
tobacconist's tutungerie f
today azi
toe deget nt de la picior
toilet paper hârtie f igienică
toilet water apă f de toaletă
toiletry parfumerie f
toilets toaleta f
tomato roșie f

tomato juice suc nt de roșii
tomb mormânt nt
tomorrow mâine
tongue limbă f
tonic water apă f tonică
tonight deseară; diseară
tonsils amigdale fpl
too prea; **(also)** de asemenea
too much prea mult
tools scule fpl
tooth dinte m
toothache durere f de dinți
toothbrush perie f de dinți
toothpaste pastă de dinți f
top, at the vârf (în vârful capului); sus
torch (flashlight) lanternă f
torn rupt
touch, to a atinge
tough (meat) (carne) tare
tour croazieră f; traseu nt
tourist office agenție f de voiaj; oficiu nt de turism
tourist tax taxă turistică f
tow truck mașină f de depanare
towards spre
towel prosop nt
towelling (terrycloth) material nt flaușat
tower turn nt
town oraș nt
town center centru nt
town hall primărie f
toy jucărie f
toy shop magazin de jucării nt
tracksuit trening nt
traffic trafic nt
traffic light semafor nt
trailer rulotă f
train tren nt
tram tramvai nt
tranquilliser tranchilizant nt
transfer (finance) transfer nt
transformer transformator nt
translate, to a traduce
transport, means of mijloace ntpl de transport
Transylvania Transilvania f
travel agency agenție f de voiaj
travel guide ghid nt

travel sickness rău nt de călătorie
travel, to a călători
traveler's cheque cec nt de voiaj; cec de călătorie
traveling bag sac m de voiaj
treatment tratament nt
tree copac m
tremendous nemaipomenit
trim, to (a beard) a aranja
trip călătorie f
trolley cărucior nt
trousers pantaloni mpl
trout păstrăv m
truck camion nt
try on, to a proba
tube tub nt
Tuesday marti f
tumbler pahar nt
turkey curcă f
Turkey Turcia f
turn, to (change direction) a (se) întoarce
turnip nap m
turquoise turcoaz; colour turcoaz
turtleneck guler nt pe gât
tweezers pensetă f
twelve doisprezece
twenty douăzeci
twice de două ori
twin beds cu două paturi
two doi
typewriter mașină f de scris
tyre cauciuc nt

U

ugly urât
Ukraine Ucraina f
umbrella umbrelă f
umbrella (beach) umbrelă f de soare
uncle unchi m
unconscious (to be) a-și pierde cunoștinta
under sub
underdone (meat) cu putin sânge
underground (railway) metrou nt
underpants chiloti mpl
undershirt maiou nt
understand, to a înțelege
undress, to a (se) dezbrăca
United States Statele Unite fpl
university universitate f

unleaded (benzină) f fără plumb
until până
up sus
upper de sus
upset stomach (a avea) stomacul nt deranjat
upstairs la etaj
urgent urgent
urine urină f
use, to a folosi
useful util
usually de obicei; obișnuit

V

V-neck cu guler nt în formă de V
vacancy liber
vacant liber
vacation vacanță f
vaccinate, to a (se) vaccina
vacuum flask termos nt
vaginal infection infecție f vaginală
valley vale f
value valoare f
value-added tax taxă f pe valoare adăugată
vanilla vanilie f
veal vitel m
vegetables legume fpl
vegetable store aprozar nt
vegetarian vegetarian
vein venă f
velvet catifea f
velveteen bumbac nt plușat
venereal disease boală f venerică
venison ăprioară f
vermouth vermut nt
very foarte
vest (Am.) vestă f
vest (Br.) maiou nt
veterinarian veterinar m
video camera cameră f video
video cassette casetă f video
video recorder aparat nt video
view (panorama) edere f
village sat nt
vinegar otet nt
vineyard vie f
visit vizită f
visit, to a vizita
visiting hours orele fpl de vizită
vitamin pill vitamine (tablete) fpl

vodka vodcă f
volleyball volei nt
voltage voltaj nt
vomit, to a vărsa

W

waist brâu nt
waistcoat vestă f
wait, to a aștepta
waiter chelner m; ospătar m
waiting room sala f de așteptare
waitress chelnerită f
wake, to a se scula
Wales Țara Galilor f
walk, to a merge
wall zid nt
wallet portmoneu nt
walnut nuc m
want, to a dori; a vrea
warm cald; fierbinte
wash, to a spăla
washable care se spală
washbasin chiuvetă f
washing-up liquid detergent nt de vase
washing powder detergent nt de rufe
watch ceas nt
watchmaker's ceasornicar m
watchstrap curea f de ceas
water apă f
water flask termos nt
water melon pepene m roșu
watercress măcriș n
waterfall cascadă f
waterproof antiacvatic
water-skis schi nautic
wave val nt
way drum nt
we noi
weather vreme f
weather forecast (ce vreme se prevede)
   prevedere f meteorologică
wedding ring verighetă f
Wednesday miercuri f
week săptămână f
weekday zi f lucrătoare
weekend sfârșit nt de săptămână
well bine
well-done (meat) bine prăjită
west vest nt

what ce
wheel roată f
when când
where unde
where from de unde
which care
whipped cream frișcă f
whisky whisky nt
white alb
who cine
whole întreg
why de ce
wick meșă f
wide larg
wide-angle lens obiectiv nt superangular
wife soție f
wig perucă f
wild boar porc m mistret
wind vânt nt
window fereastră f; (shop) vitrină f
windscreen/shield parbriz nt
windsurfer windsurfer m
wine vin nt
wine list listă de vinuri f
wine merchant's magazin nt de vinuri
winter iarnă f
winter sports sporturi ntpl de iarnă
wiper (car) ștergătoare nt de parbriz
wish urare f
with cu
withdraw, to (from account) a scoate
withdrawal restituire f
without fără
woman femeie f
wonderful minunat
wood pădure f
wool lână f
word cuvânt nt
work, to a funcționa
working day zi f lucrătoare
worse mai rău
worsted lână toarsă f
wound rană f
wrap up, to a împacheta
wrinkle-free neșifonat
wristwatch ceas nt de mână
write, to a scrie
writing pad bloc nt notes

writing paper hârtie de scris f
wrong greşit; rău

X

X-ray radiografie f

Y

year an nt
yellow galben
yes da
yesterday ieri
yet încă

yoghurt iaurt nt
you tu, dumneavoastră
young tînăr m
your a ta, al tău, a/al dumneavoastră
youth hostel cămin nt; cazare f

Z

zero zero
zip(per) fermoar nt
zoo grădină f zoologică
zoology zoologie f
zucchini dovlecel m

Romanian–English

A

a (se) dezbrăca undress, to
a (se) întoarce turn, to (change direction)
a (se) răni injure, to
a (se) umfla swell, to
a (se) vaccina vaccinate, to
a şti know, to
a aştepta expect, to
a aştepta wait, to
a accepta accept, to
a aduce bring, to
a ajunge get to, to
a ajunge to get (go)
a ajuta help, to
a anula cancel, to
a aranja trim, to (a beard)
a arăta point, to
a arăta show, to
a asculta listen, to
a atinge touch, to
a avea have, to
a avea nevoie de need, to
a avea o pană de motor break down, to
a bea drink, to
a cădea fall, to
a călători travel, to
a călca iron, to
a călca press, to (iron)
a campa camp, to
a cânta sing, to
a cânta; a juca play, to

a căuta look for, to
a ceda (trecerea) give way, to (traffic)
a cheltui spend, to
a cina f; a lua masa de seară dinner (have)
a ciocăni knock, to
a coase sew, to
a coase stitch, to
a coborî get off, to
a comanda order, to (goods, meal)
a comanda to get (fetch)
a completa fill in, to
a conduce drive, to
a confirma confirm, to
a construi build, to
a contine contain, to
a costa cost, to
a crede think, to (believe)
a cumpăra buy, to
a curge drip, to
a curge sânge din nas nosebleed
a da place, to
a da un telefon personal call/person-to-person call
a da; a chema call, to (summon)
a da; a pune give, to
a dansa dance, to
a datora owe, to
a declara declare, to (customs)
a depăşi overtake, to
a deranja disturb, to
a deschide open, to

a **developa** develop, to
a **dori; a vrea** want, to
a **dormi** sleep, to
a **durea** hurt, to
a **ei** her
a **face** do, to
a **face** make, to
a **face** make up, to *(prepare)*
a **face autostop** hitchhike, to
a **face loc** get past, to
a **fi interesat** interested, to be
a **folosi** use, to
a **fuma** smoke, to
a **functiona** work, to
a **fura** steal, to
a **găsi** find, to
a **ieşi** go out, to
a **împacheta** wrap up, to
a **împinge** push, to
a **înştiinţa** notify, to
a **încălzi** heat, to
a **încălzi peste măsură** overheat, to *(engine)*
a **încasa** cash, to
a **începe** start, to
a **închide** close, to
a **închiria** hire, to
a **închiria** let, to *(hire out)*
a **închiria** rent, to
a **include** include, to
a **îndruma** direct, to
a **înghiţi** swallow, to
a **înota** swim, to
a **înregistra** register, to *(luggage)*
a **înregistra bagajele** check in, to *(airport)*
a **însemna** mean, to
a **întâlni** meet, to
a **înţelege** understand, to
a **înţepa** sting, to
a **intra la apă** shrink, to
a **întrerupe** cut off, to *(interrupt)*
a **invita** invite, to
a **îţi fi sete** thirsty, to be
a **juca** perform, to *(theater)*
a **lipsi** miss, to
a **livra** deliver, to
a **locui** live, to
a **lua** get, to *(find)*
a **lua** pick up, to *(person)*
a **lua; a merge;** *(time)* **a dura**take, to

a **lui** his
a **mânca** eat, to
a **mări** enlarge, to
a **măsura** measure, to
a **merge** go, to
a **merge** walk, to
a **mişca** move, to
a **modifica** alter, to *(garment)*
a **multumi** thank, to
a **obtine; a cumpăra** to get *(obtain)*
a **opri; a sta** stop, to
a **parca** park, to
a **permite** may *(can)*
a **pescui** fishing
a **picta** paint, to
a **pierde** lose, to
a **plăti** pay, to
a **plăti; a retine** charge, to
a **pleca, a părăsi** check out, to
a **plonja** skin-diving
a **ploua** rain, to
a **potrivi** match, to *(colour)*
a **prescrie** prescribe, to
a **prezenta** introduce, to
a **proba** fit, to
a **proba** try on, to
a **pronunta** pronounce, to
a **puna la dispozitie** provide, to
a **pune** put, to
a **pune la poştă** mail, to
a **pune la poştă** post, to
a **pune un petec** patch, to *(clothes)*
a **putea să** can *(be able to)*
a **râde** laugh, to
a **rămâne în urmă** late, to be
a **raporta** report, to *(a theft)*
a **recomanda** recommend, to
a **reduce viteza** slow down, to
a **repara** mend, to
a **repara** repair
a **repara** repair, to
a **repeta** repeat, to
a **respira** breathe, to
a **rezerva** reserve, to
a **rotunji** round up, to
a **schia** ski, to
a **schimba** exchange, to
a **schimba; bani ntpl mărunti**change, to
a **scoate** withdraw, to

(from account)
a scrie write, to
a se arde burn out, to *(bulb)*
a se bloca jam, to
a se da jos din pat get up, to
a se distra enjoy oneself, to
a se grăbi hurry, to be in a
a se întinde lie down, to
a se întoarce go back, to
a se întoarce;
înapoia return, to *(come back)*
a se scrie spell, to
a se scula wake, to
a se uita look, to
a se zice; (phone) a telefonacall, to *(give name)*
a semna sign, to
a simți feel, to *(physical state)*
a spăla clean, to
a spăla wash, to
a sparge; a rupe break, to
a spera hope, to
a spune tell, to
a sta jos sit down, to
a sta; (reside) a locui stay, to
a studia study, to
a suna ring, to *(doorbell)*
a suna înapoi call back, to
a ta, al tău, a/al dumneavoastrăyour
a telefona telephone, to *(call)*
a tine keep, to
a traduce translate, to
a trage; (tooth) a extrage pull, to
a trata fix, to
a trebui, a fi necesar have to, to *(must)*
a trebui; avea nevoie; a credemust *(have to)*
a trece pass, to *(driving)*
a trece pass through, to
a trimite un telex telex, to
a trimite; a livra; a expediasend, to
a tuși cough, to
a tunde cut, to *(with scissors)*
a uita forget, to
a urma follow, to
a vărsa vomit, to
a vedea; a întâlni see, to
a verifica; a controla; (luggage) a înregistra check, to
a vinde sell, to
a vizita visit, to

a vorbi speak, to
a vrea; (please) a plăcea like, to
a-și pierde cunoștința unconscious (to be)
așteptati hold on! *(phone)*
abces *nt* abscess
abreviere *nt* abbreviation
ac de păr *nt* hairpin
ac *nt* needle
ac *nt* de cravată tie pin
ac *nt* de siguranță safety pin
ac *nt*; agrafă *f* pin
accesorii *nplt* accessories
accident *nt* accident
aceștia *mpl*; acestea *fpl* these
acela that
același same
acelea those
acest it
achizitie *f* purchase
acolo there
actiune *f* share *(finance)*
acum now
adânc deep
adaptor *nt* adaptor
admis admitted
adresă *f* address
adresa *f* de acasă home address
aduce bring down, to a
aer *nt* conditionat air conditioning
aeroport *nt* airport
afaceri *fpl* business
afară outside
afină *f* bilberry
afină *f* blueberry
Africa de Sud *f* South Africa
Africa *f* Africa
afumat smoked
agendă *f* de adrese address book
agenție *f* de închiriat mașini car rental
agenție *f* de voiaj booking office
agenție *f* de voiaj travel agency
agenție *f* de voiaj; oficiu *nt* de turism tourist office
agrafă *f* bobby pin
agrafă *f* pentru hârtie paperclip
agrișe *fpl* gooseberries
aici here
ajunge; a veni; a sosi arrive, to a
ajutor help!

al şaptelea seventh
al şaselea sixth
al cincilea fifth
al doilea; secundă f second
al lor their
al meu my
al nostru our
al nouălea ninth
al optulea eighth
al patrulea fourth
al său, a sa, ai săi, ale sale its
al treilea third
al zecelea tenth
alb white
alb-negru black and white (film)
albastru blue
alcool nt alcohol
alcoolic alcoholic
alergic allergic
alergie f **la polen** hay fever
alfabet nt alphabet
aliaj nt **cu cositor** pewter
alpinism nt mountaineering
alt other
altul m; **alta** f another
alune fpl **de pădure** hazelnut
amabil kind
amar bitter
ambasadă f embassy
America de Nord f North America
America de Sud South America
american m American
ametist nt amethyst
ameţit dizzy
amigdale fpl tonsils
amplificator nt amplifier
an bisect m leap year
an nt year
ananas m pineapple
anason nt aniseed
andive fpl chicory
anestetic nt anaesthetic
anghinare f artichoke
Anglia f England
animal nt animal
anotimp nt season
antiacvatic waterproof
antibiotic nt antibiotic

antichităţi fpl antiques
anticoncepţionale ntpl contraceptives
antidepresiv nt antidepressant
antreu nt appetizer
antreu nt starter (meal)
anuar nt directory (phone)
anuar nt **telefonic** telephone directory
Anul Nou m New Year
anunţ nt notice (sign)
apă f water
apă f **caldă** hot water
apă f **curentă** running water
apă f **de gură** mouthwash
apă f **de toaletă** toilet water
apă f **gazoasă** carbonated (fizzy)
apă f **minerală** mineral water
apă f **potabilă** drinking water
apă f **tonică** tonic water
aparat nt de filmat; aparat de fotografiat camera
aparat nt **de ras** razor
aparat nt **de ras** shaver
aparat nt **video** video recorder
aparatură f appliance
aparatură f **electrică** electrical appliance
apartament nt apartment
apartament nt flat (apartment)
apel nt **telefonic** call (phone)
apel nt **telefonic** telephone call
apendice nt appendix
apendicită f appendicitis
aperitiv nt aperitif
aprilie m April
aproape; lângă near
aprozar nt greengrocer's
aprozar nt vegetable store
arahidă f peanut
argint nt; (colour) **argintiu** silver
argintărie f silverware
arheologie f archaeology
arhitect m architect
arpagic nt chives
arsură f burn
arsură f **de soare** sunburn
artă f art
arte fpl **frumoase** fine arts
articol nt **de uz casnic** household article
artificial artificial

tist *m* artist
tizanat *nt* handicrafts
scuţitoare *f* pencil sharpener
sia Asia
sigurare *f* insurance
sigurare *f* **casco** full insurance
sistentă *f* **rutieră** road assistance
spirină *f* aspirin
sta; acesta this
stmă *f* asthma
tă *f* thread
tac *nt* **de cord** heart attack
telier *nt* **de fotografiat** photographer
tenţie look out!
tenţie *f* caution
tunci then
ugust *m* August
ur *nt* gold
urit gold plated
uriu golden
ustralia Australia
ustria Austria
utobuz *nt* bus
utocar *nt* coach *(bus)*
utomat *nt* automatic
utostradă *f* expressway
utostradă *f* motorway
vion *nt* airplane
vion *nt* plane
zi today

ăşică *f* blister
ac *nt* ferry
ăcănie *f* grocery *(grocer's)*
agaj *nt* baggage
agaj *nt* luggage
ăiat *m* boy
ăiat *m* son
aie *f* bath
aie *f* bathroom
alanţă *f* balance *(finance)*
alcon *nt* balcony
alcon *nt* circle *(theatre)*
alcon *nt* mezzanine *(theatre)*
alet *nt* ballet
anană *f* banana
ancă *f* bank *(finance)*
ancnotă *f* banknote

bancnotă *f* note *(banknote)*
bandaj *nt* bandage
bandaj *nt* **elastic** elastic bandage
bani *mpl* money
bar *nt* bar *(room)*
barbă *f* beard
bărbat *m*; **om** *m* man
bărbaţi *mpl* gentlemen
barcă *f* boat
barcă *f* **cu motor** motorboat
barcă *f* **cu pânze** sailing boat
barcă *f* **cu rame** rowing boat
barcă *f* **de salvare** life boat
baschet *nt* basketball
bătătură *f* corn *(foot)*
baterie *f* battery
batist *nt* cambric
batistă de hârtie *f* tissue *(handkerchief)*
batistă *f* handkerchief
baton *nt* **de ciocolată** chocolate bar
băutură *f* drink
băutură *f* **răcoritoare** soft drink
băutură *f* **simplă** straight *(drink)*
bec *nt* bulb *(light)*
bej beige
Belgia Belgium
benzină *f* gasoline
benzină *f* petrol
benzină *f* super premium *(gasoline)*
bere *f* beer
biban *m* perch
biberon *nt* feeding bottle
bibliotecă *f* library
bicicletă *f* bicycle
Bielorusia *f* Belorus
bigudiu *nt* curler
bigudiuri *ntpl* set *(hair)*
bilet *nt* ticket
bilet *nt* **dus-întors** return ticket
bilet *nt* **dus-întors** round-trip ticket
bine fine *(OK)*
bine right *(correct)*
bine well
bine făcut, potrivit medium *(meat)*
bine prăjită well-done *(meat)*
binoclu *nt* binoculars
birou *n* **de schimb** currency exchange office
birou *nt* office

birou *nt* **de bagaje** left-luggage office
birou *nt* **de bagaje; înregistrarea** *f* **bagajelor** baggage check
birou *nt* **de obiecte pierdute** lost and found/ lost property office
birou *nt* **de rezervări** reservations office
birou PTT *nt* telegraph office
biscuit *nt* biscuit *(Br.)*
biserică *f* church
blănărie *f* furrier's
blitz *nt* flash *(photography)*
bloc *nt* notes writing pad
blugi *mpl* jeans
bluză *f* blouse
bluză *f* **de trening din bumbac** sweatshirt
boală *f* disease
boală *f* illness
boală *f* sickness *(illness)*
bobină *f* **de film** roll film
bolnav *m* sick *(ill)*
bolnav *m*, **bolnavă** *f* ill
borcan *nt* jar *(container)*
botanică *f* botany
box *nt* boxing
brânză *f* cheese
brat *nt* arm
brățară *f* bangle
brățară *f* bracelet
brățară *f* **cu talismanuri** charm bracelet
brățară *f* **lănțișor** chain bracelet
brâu *nt* waist
bretele *fpl* braces *(suspenders)*
bretele *fpl* suspenders *(Am.)*
breton *nt* bangs
breton *nt* fringe
briceag *m* penknife
brichetă *f* cigarette lighter
brichetă *f* lighter
britanic *m* British
broșă *f* brooch
brodat embroidered
broderie *f* embroidery
brutărie *f* baker's
buiotă *f* **cu apă fierbinte** hot-water bottle
bujie *f* spark(ing) plug
Bulgaria *f* Bulgaria
bumbac *nt* cotton
bumbac *nt* **plușat** velveteen

bun good
bună hi
bună dimineata good morning
bună seara good evening
bună ziua good afternoon
bună; *(telephone)* **alo** hello
burete *m* sponge
bursă *f* stock exchange
burtieră *f* panty girdle
busolă *f* compass
busuioc *nt* basil
buton *nt* **de manșetă** cuff link
buton *nt*, **întrerupător** *nt* switch (electric)
buză *f* lip
buzunar *nt* pocket

C

ca like
căști *fpl* headphones
cabană *f* cabana
cabină de bagaje *f;* **birou** *nt* **de bagaje** luggage locker
cabină *f* cabin (ship)
cabină *f* **de bagaje; birou** *nt* **de bagaje** baggage locker
cabină *f* **de probă** fitting room
cabină *f* **de schimb** bathing hut
cabină *f* **pentru o persoană** single cabin
cabinet *nt* **medical** doctor's office
cabinet *nt* **medical** surgery (consulting room)
cadou *nt* gift
cadou *nt* present
cafe-bar *nt* café
cafea *f* coffee
cafea *f* **neagră (turcească)** black coffee
caiet *nt* exercise book
câine *m* dog
caisă *f* apricot
călărie *f* horseback riding
călătorie *f* journey
călătorie *f* trip
calculator *nt* calculator
calculator *nt* **de buzunar** pocket calculator
cald; fierbinte warm
cale ferată *f* railway
calendar *nt* calendar
calitate *f* quality
calmant *nt* analgesic
calmant *nt* painkiller

maşă *f* shirt
maşă *f* T-shirt
meră *f* room
meră *f* **cu un pat** single room
meră *f* **de două persoane** double room
meră *f* **de filmat** cine camera
meră *f* **de filmat** movie camera
meră *f* **video** video camera
meristă *f* maid
mion *nt* truck
mp *nt* field
mping *nt* camping
mping *nt*; **loc nt de campare** camp site
nă *f* mug
nada *f* Canada
nadian *m* Canadian
nd when
ntec *nt* song
ntitate *f* quantity
p *nt* head
pşună *f* strawberry
pelă *f* chapel
pere *fpl* capers
pital *nt* capital (finance)
pot *nt* dressing gown
prioară *f* venison
psă *f* press stud
psă *f* snap fastener
psă *f* staple
rafă *f* carafe
rat *nt* carat
rbune *nt* **pentru grătar** charcoal
rburator *nt* carburettor
rcel *m* cramp
re which
riocă *nt* felt-tip pen
rlig *nt* **de cort** peg (tent)
rlig *nt* **de cort** tent peg
rlig *nt* **de rufe** clothes peg/pin
rnaţi *mpl* sausage
rne *f* meat
rnet *nt* notebook
rnet *nt* **de bilete** booklet (of tickets)
rnet *nt* **de conducere** driving licence
rnet *nt* **de conducere** licence (driving)
rpetă *f* carpet
rte *f* book
rte *f* paperback

carte *f* **de credit** credit card
carte *f* **de gramatică** grammar book
carte *f* **de joc** *f*; **carte** *f* **de visita** card
cărţi *fpl* **de joc,** playing card
cartof *m* potato
cartofi mpl cipşi crisps
cartofi mpl prăjiti chips
cartuş *nt* **de ţigări; pachet** *nt* **de**
  ţigări carton (of cigarettes)
cărucior *nt* cart
cărucior *nt* trolley
cărucior *nt* de bagaje baggage cart
cărucior *nt* **de bagaje** luggage trolley
casă *f* home
casă *f* house
casă f de bilete ticket office
căsătorit married
cască *f* **de înot** bathing cap
cascadă *f* waterfall
casetă *f* cassette
casetă *f* **video** video cassette
casetofon *nt* cassette recorder
casetofon *nt* tape recorder
castană *f* chestnut
castel *nt* castle
castravete *m* cucumber
castravete m murat gherkin
cât how much
cât de departe how far
cât timp how long
catalog nt catalogue
cataramă f buckle
catedrală f cathedral
câţi mpl, câte fpl how many
catifea f velvet
catolic Catholic
cauciuc nt rubber (material)
cauciuc nt tyre
cazare şi micul dejun bed and breakfast
ce what
ceaşcă f cup
ceai nt tea
ceai nt de plante medicinale herb tea
ceai nt rece iced tea
ceapă f onion
ceas nt clock
ceas nt watch
ceas nt de buzunar pocket watch

ceas nt de mână wristwatch
ceas nt digital digital
ceasornicar m watchmaker's
ceată f fog
cec nt check (Am.)
cec nt cheque
cec nt personal personal cheque
cel mai aproape nearest
cel puţin at least
celulă f fotoelectrică light meter
center centru nt town
centimetru m centimetre
centrala f operator
centru nt centre
centru nt downtown
centru nt comercial shopping area
centru nt comercial shopping centre
centrul nt oraşului city centre
centură f girdle
cer nt sky
ceramică f ceramics
cercel m earring
cereală f cereal
cerneală f ink
certificat nt certificate
certificat nt medical medical certificate
cerut required
cetate f fortress
ceva something
ceva; nimic anything
cheie f key
chelner m; ospătar m waiter
chelneriţă f waitress
cheltuieli fplexpenses
**cheque cec nt de voiaj; cec de
   călătorie**traveller's
chibrit nt, match (matchstick)
chiflă f roll
chiftele fpl meatball
chihlimbar ntamber
chiloţi mpl panties
chiloti mpl underpants
chimen m caraway
China f China
chioşc nt cu gustări snack bar
chioşc nt de ziare newsagent's
chioşc nt de ziare newsstand
chitanţă f receipt

chiuvetă f washbasin
ciclism nt cycling
ciclu nt period (monthly)
cimbru m thyme
cimitir nt cemetery
cinci five
cincisprezecefifteen
cincizeci fifty
cine who
cinema nt cinema
cineva anyone
cineva someone
ciocan nt hammer
ciocan nt mallet
ciocolată f chocolate
ciorap m stocking
ciorapi mpl cu chilot panty hose
cireşe fpl cherry
cistită f cystitis
ciupercă f mushroom
cizmă f boot
cizmar m shoemaker's
clădire f building
clădirea f parlamentului parliament
   building
clamă f clip
clamă f hairgrip
clamă f de cravată tie clip
clasa f a douasecond class
clasa f business business class
clasa f întâi first class
clasic classical
clei nt paste (glue)
coş nt de picnic picnic basket
coacăz nt negru blackcurrant
coada f rear
coafor nt hairdresser
coapsă f thigh
coastă f rib
cocteil nt de fructe fruit cocktail
colac nt de salvare life belt
colant adhesive
colet nt parcel
colier nt necklace
coloană f vertebrală spine
colt nt corner
comandă f order (goods, meal)
comedie f comedy

comedie f muzicală musical
comision nt commission (fee)
compact disc nt compact disc
companie f de asigurări insurance company
concert nt concert
condiment ntspice
condimente ntpl seasoning
confirmare f confirmation
conopidă f cauliflower
consignație f second-hand shop
constipație f constipation
consulat nt consulate
cont nt bancar account
contagios contagious
contract nt contract
control nt control
convorbire f cu taxă inversă collect call
copac m tree
copil m baby
copil m child
copt baked
coral m coral
corn porumb m sweet
corp nt body
cort nt tent
cost nt rate (price)
cost nt aproximativ; pret nt estimativ estimate (cost)
cost nt; tarif nt; taxă f charge
costul nt (biletului) fare (ticket)
costul nt prin poștă postage
costum nt bărbătesc; suit (man's)
costum nt de damă suit (woman's)
costum nt de baie bathing suit
costum nt de baie swimming trunks
costum nt de înot swimsuit
cotlet nt chop (meat)
cotlet nt cutlet
crab m crab
Crăciun nt Christmas
crap m carp
cratiță f saucepan
cravată f tie
credit nt credit
creion nt crayon
creion nt pencil
creion nt de sprâncene eyebrow pencil
creion nt mechanic mechanical pencil

creion nt mecanic propelling pencil
cremă f cream (toiletry)
cremă f antiseptică antiseptic cream
cremă f de bronzat sun-tan cream
cremă f de mâini hand cream
cremă f de noapte night cream
cremă f de pantofi shoe polish
cremă f de picioare foot cream
cremă f de ras shaving cream
cremă f hidratantă moisturizing cream
crep crepe
crevete m shrimp
cristal nt crystal
croazieră f cruise
croazieră f river trip
croazieră f; traseu nt tour
croitor m tailor's
crom nt chromium
cruce f cross
crudă; în sânge rare (meat)
cu with
cu două paturi twin beds
cu filtru filter-tipped
cu guler nt în formă de V V-neck
cu putin sânge underdone (meat)
cușetă de dormit f berth
cuart nt quartz
cuburi ntpl building blocks/bricks
cuburi ntpl de gheață ice cube
cuișoare fpl clove
culoare f shade (color)
culoare f; color
cupru nt copper
curând soon
curat clean
curățătorie f dry cleaner's
curbă f bend (road)
curbă f curve (road)
curcă f turkey
curea f belt
curea f de ceas watchstrap
curea f de ventilator fan belt
curent common (frequent)
curent nt de apă current
curmale fpl date (fruit)
curs nt de schimb exchange rate
curse fpl de cai horse racing
cutie f box

cutie f de bijuterii jewel box
cutie f de conservă can (container)
cutie f de conservă tin (container)
cutie f de culori paintbox
cutie f de scrisori mailbox
cutie f poştală letter box
cuţit nt knife
cuvânt nt word
da yes
dacă if
Danemarca f Denmark
dans nt dance
dantelă f lace
dar but
dată f date (day)

D

de asemenea also, too
de capacitate medie medium-sized
de ce why
de două ori twice
de jos lower
de la from
de luat acasă take away, to
de obicei; obişnuit usually
de persoană per person
de spălat de mână hand washable
de sus upper
de unde where from
de urgenţă special delivery
de, din since
deal nt hill
deasupra above
decât than
decembrie m December
deceniu nt decade
decizie f decision
declanşator nt cable release
decofeinizat decaffeinated
decolorant nt bleach
dedesubt below
deget nt finger
deget nt de la picior toe
degetul nt mare thumb
dejun nt; **masa** f lunch
demipensiune f half board
demipensiune f modified American plan
dentist m dentist

deodorant nt deodorant
departament nt; (shop) raion nt departme[...]
(museum)
departe far
depunere f; avans nt deposit (down
payment)
deranjat; nu funcţionează out of order
deschis open
deschizător n de conserve t can opener
deschizător nt de conserve tin opener
deschizător nt de sticle bottle-opener
deseară; diseară tonight
desert nt dessert
desinfectant nt disinfectant
desk casă f cash
destul enough
detergent de rufe washing powder
detergent nt de vase dishwashing deterger[...]
detergent nt de vase washing-up liquid
developat processing (photo)
deviere f detour (traffic)
deviere f diversion (traffic)
devreme early
diabetic diabetic
diamant nt diamond
diapozitiv nt slide (photo)
diapozitiv nt color colour slide
diaree f diarrhoea
dicţionar nt dictionary
dificultate f difficulty
difuzor nt speaker (loudspeaker)
dimineaţa morning, in the
din nou again
dinte m tooth
direct direct
direcţie f direction
director m manager
dirijor m conductor (orchestra)
disc nt disc
disc nt record (disc)
discotecă f discotheque
disease boală f venerică venereal
dislocat dislocated
dispozitiv nt de curăţat pipă pipe tool
dispozitiv nt de numărătoare exposure
counter
diverse miscellaneous
doamna f Mrs.

doar just (only)
dobândă f interest (finance)
doc nt denim
doctor m doctor
doctor pediatru m children's doctor
doi two
doisprezece twelve
dolar m dollar
domnişoară f Miss
domnul m Mr.
două săptămâni fortnight
douăzeci twenty
dovlecel m courgette
dovlecel m zucchini
drăguț pretty
dreapta right (direction)
drept înainte straight ahead
dresuri ntpl tights
dropsuri ntpl candy
drum nt road
drum nt way
duş nt shower
dulce sweet
dulciuri ntpl sweet (confectionery)
duminică f Sunday
după after
după-amiaza f afternoon, in the
dur hard
durabilă sturdy
durere de cap f headache
durere f ache
durere f pain
durere f **de burtă** stomach ache
durere f **de ceafă** stiff neck
durere f **de dinti** toothache
durere f **de gât** sore throat
durere f **de spate** backache
durere f **de urechi** earache
dureri fpl **la ciclu** period pains
dureros sore (painful)
duzină f dozen

E

ea she
echipă f team
echipament nt equipment
echipament nt **de camping** camping equipment
echipament nt **de plonjat** skin-diving equipment
echipament nt **de schi** skiing equipment
egzemă f rash
ei mpl; **ele** fpl they
el he
electric(e) electric(al)
electricitate f electricity
electronic electronic
Elveția f Switzerland
email nt enamel
englez; englezesc English
escalator nt; **lift** nt escalator
est nt east
etichetă f label
eurocec nt Eurocheque
Europa f Europe
examen nt **medical** check-up (medical)
excursie f excursion
excursie f sightseeing
expoziție f exhibition
expres (tren) nt express
expresie f expression
expunere f exposure (photography)

F

factură f invoice
făină f flour
făinoase fpl pasta paste
familie f family
fântână f fountain
fără without
fără mâneci sleeveless
fard nt **de pleope** eye shadow
farfurie f plate
farfurioară f saucer
farmacie f chemist's
farmacie f drugstore
farmacie f pharmacy
fasole f bean
fasole f **fideluța** French bean
fasole verde f green bean
fată f daughter
față f face
fată f girl
fax nt fax
fazan m pheasant
febră f fever
februarie m February
fel nt kind (type)

fel nt sort (kind)
felicitări fpl congratulation
felie f slice
felinar nt lantern
femei fpl ladies
femeie f woman
fereastră f; (shop) vitrină f window
fericit happy
fericit merry
fermă f farm
fermoar nt zip(per)
fetru nt felt
fibe, to a
ficat m liver
fiecare each
fier nt de călcat iron (for laundry)
fierărie f ironmonger's
fierbinte hot cald; (boiling)
fiert boiled
fiert stewed
fiert în apă poached
fiert înăbușit braised
fildeș nt ivory
film m movie
film nt film
filme ntpl movies
filtru nt filter
Finlanda f Finland
fixativ nt setting lotion
fixativ nt de păr hair spray
flanelă f flannel
floare f flower
florărie f florist's
foame f hungry
foarfece nt de unghii nail scissors
foarfece nt de unghii cu arc nail clippers
foarfece nt; foarfecă f scissors
foarte very
foc nt fire
foc nt light (for cigarette)
folie f de mușama groundsheet
fond de ten nt foundation cosmetic
formular nt form (document)
formular nt de asigurare health insurance form
formular nt de înregistrare registration form
fotbal n football

fotbal nt soccer
fotocopie f photocopy
fotografie f photography
fotografie f de pașaport passport photo
fowl bibilică f guinea
frână f brake
frânghie f rope
Franța f France
frate m brother
frază f phrase
frișcă f cream
frișcă f whipped cream
friptură f de vacă roast beef
frisoane npl shivery
frizer m barber's
fruct nt fruit
fructe ntpl de mare seafood
frumos beautiful
frumos lovely
frumos nice (beautiful)
fular nt scarf
fulger nt lightning
fumător m smoker
fumuriu tinted
furculiță f fork
fursec n cookie
furt nt theft
furtună f thunderstorm
furuncul m boil
fustă f skirt

G
gabardină f gabardine
galben yellow
găleată f bucket
galerie f de artă art gallery
galerie f de artă gallery
găletică f pail
gară f railway station
gară f station (railway)
garaj nt; servis nt garage
garderoba f cloakroom
gâscă f goose
gastrită f gastritis
gât nt neck
gât nt throat
gata ready
gaură f hole
gaz nt gas

gaz nt kerosene
gaz nt butan; **butelie f de gaz** butane gas
gaz nt **de brichetă** lighter fluid/gas
geantă f frigorifică cool box
geantă f; poșeta f handbag
gel nt de păr hair gel
gem nt jam (preserves)
genitale ntpl genitals organe
genunchi m ankle
genunchi m knee
geologie f geology
ger nt frost
Germania f Germany
gheață f ice
ghete fpl de schi ski boot
ghișeu nt counter
ghid nt guide
ghid nt guidebook
ghid nt travel guide
ghid nt al hotelurilor hotel directory/guide
ghimber m ginger
gin cu apă tonică gin and tonic
gin nt gin
ginecolog m gynaecologist
gingie f gum (teeth)
gips nt plaster
glandă f gland
gol empty
golf nt golf
grad nt degree (temperature)
grădină f garden
grădină f botanică botanical gardens
grădina f publică gardens
grădină f zoologică zoo
gram nt gram(me)
gramatică f grammar
gras fat (meat)
grătar nt grilled
grav seriously
gravidă f pregnant
greșeală f mistake
greșit; rău wrong
greață f nausea
Grecia f Greece
grepfrut nt grapefruit
greu difficult
greu; *puternic heavy*
gri grey

gri grey
gripă f flu
gripă f influenza
groaznic; urât awful
grup nt group
guler nt collar
guler nt pe gât turtleneck
gumă f eraser
gumă f rubber (eraser)
gumă f de mestecat chewing gum
gură f mouth
gustare f snack

H

haină f coat
haină f de ploaie raincoat
haine fpl clothes
halat nt de baie bathrobe
hamac nt hammock
hamal m; portar m porter
hanorac nt anorak
hartă f map
harta f drumurilor road map
harta f străzilor; harta orașului street map
hârtie de scris f writing paper
hârtie f paper
hârtie f de desenat drawing paper
hârtie f de scris notepaper
hârtie f igienică toilet paper
hârtie f indigou carbon paper
helicopter nt helicopter
hipodrom nt race course/track
homar m lobster
hostel cămin nt; cazare f youth
hot m thief
hotel nt hotel
hotel-pensiune nt guesthouse
hoții! stop thief!

I

ianuarie m January
iarnă f winter
iaurt nt yoghurt
iaz nt pond
icoană f icon
icter nt jaundice
ieșire f exit
ieșire f de incendiu emergency exit
ieftin cheap

iepure m hare
iepure m rabbit
ieri yesterday
îmbrăcăminte f clothing
imediat at once
important important
important; principal main
importat imported
impresionant impressive
în in
în aburi steamed
în afara sezonului low season
în apropiere nearby
în are liber open-air
în jur de around (approximately)
în medie average
in nt linen (cloth)
în plus extra
în sezon high season
în timpul during
în urmă cu; acum (doi ani) ago (two years)
înainte before (time)
înălțime f height
înălțime f; mare high
înapoi; în spate behind
înăuntru inside
încă yet
încărcător nt de film cartridge (camera)
începător m beginner
început nt beginning
încheietură f joint
închiriere f hire
închiriere f rental
închirieri fpl auto car hire
închis shut
inclus included
India f India
indigestie f indigestion
inel nt ring (jewelery)
inel nt cu sigiliu signet ring
inel nt de logodnă engagement ring
infectat infected
infecție f infection
infecție f vaginală vaginal infection
inflamație f inflammation
inflație f inflation
informație f information
informație f inquiry
înfundat blocked

înghețată f ice cream
îngrijitoare f de copii, babysitter f
  babysitter
îngrozitor terrifying
inimă f heart
injecție f injection
înot nt swimming
înregistrare f registration
insecticid nt insect spray
insolatie f sunstroke
instrument nt muzical instrument (musical
instrument nt pentru curățat pipa pipe
  cleaner
întâlnire f date (appointment)
întârziere f delay
înțepătură f sting
înțepătură f de insectă insect bite
interesant interesting
interior nt extension (phone)
international international
interpret m interpreter
intersecție f crossroads
intersecție f intersection
interzis forbidden
intestin nt bowel
intoxicatie f alimentară food poisoning
intoxicatie f (alimentară) poisoning
intrare f admission
intrare f entrance
intrare f entrance fee
între between
întrebare f question
întreg whole
întuneric; închis dark
investiție f investment
invitație f invitation
iod nt iodine
ipotecă f mortgage
Irlanda f Ireland
irlandez m Irish
istorie f history
Italia f Italy
iulie m July
iunie m June
izvor nt spring (water)

J
jachetă f cardigan
jachetă f jacket

jad nt jade
jaluzea f blind (window shade)
Japonia f Japan
jazz nt jazz
jerseu nt jersey
joc de cărti nt card game
joc nt game
joc nt de şah chess set
joi f Thursday
josdown
jos nt bottom
jucărie f toy
julitură f graze
jumătate f half
jumătate de oră half an hour
jumătate f de preţ half price
jupon nt slip (underwear)

K
kilogram nt kilo(gram)
kilometraj nt mileage
kilometru m kilometre

L
la prep at
la amiază f noon
la etaj upstairs
la noapte night, at
la revedere good-bye
la ţară countryside
la timp on time
lac nt lake
lamă f blade
lamă f de rasrazor blades
lămâie f lemon
lampă f lamp
lampă f de citit reading lamp
lână f wool
lângă next to
lanternă f flashlight
lanternă f torch (flashlight)
lănţişor nt chain (jewelery)
lapte demachiant nt cleansing cream
lapte nt milk
larg wide
largi loose (clothes)
laxativ nt laxative
lecţie f lesson
lecţii fpl de schi skiing lessons

legătură f cable
legătură f de blitz lash attachment
legătură f de tren connection (transport)
legume fpl vegetables
lentilă f lens (glasses)
lentile fpl de contact contact lens
lentile fpl flexibile soft (lens)
leucoplast nt pentru bătături corn plaster
liber taken (occupied)
liber vacancy
liber vacant
liber; gratuitfree
librărie f bookshop
lichid nt fluid
lichid nt de frână brake fluid
lichior nt liqueur
lift nt elevator
lift nt lift (elevator)
limbă f language
limbă f tongue
limonadă f lemonade
lingură f spoon
linguriţă f teaspoon
linişte f quiet
liniştit calm
linie f ruler (for measuring)
linte f lentils
lipici nt glue
liră f sterlinăpound
listă de vinuri f wine list
litru nt litre
livrare f delivery
loc nt compartment (train)
loc nt place
loc nt seat
loc nt la culoar aisle seat
local nt local
locul nt naşterii place of birth
lopăţică f shovel
lopăţică f spade
loţiune f lotion
loţiune f astringentă astringent
loţiune f de păr hair lotion
loţiune f după ras aftershave lotion
lucrat de mână handmade
lumânare f candle
lumină f light (lamp)
lumină f artificială artificial light

lumină f de zi daylight
lună f month
lună f moon
lung long
luni Monday
luxat sprained

M

m de medicină generală; generalist mgeneral practitioner doctor
mașina f car
mașină f de depanare breakdown van
mașină f de depanare tow truck
mașină f de scris typewriter
măcelărie f butcher's
machiaj nt make-up
măcriș n watercress
macrou n mackerel
magazin de jucării nt toy shop
magazin nt shop
magazin nt store (shop)
magazin nt **alimentar** supermarket
magazin nt **cu articole de sport**sporting goods shop
magazin nt **cu autoservire** self-service shop
magazin nt **de antichități** antique shop
magazin nt **de aparate electrice**electrical goods shop
magazin nt **de aparate** fotocamera shop
magazin nt **de bijuterii; bijuterie** f jeweler's
magazin nt **de brânzeturi și lactate** dairy
magazin nt **de delicatese** delicatessen
magazin nt **de dulciuri** sweet shop
magazin nt **de încaltaminte** shoe shop
magazin nt **de suveniruri** souvenir shop
magazin nt **de vinuri** wine merchant's
magazin universal nt department store
măghiran nt marjoram
magnific magnificent
mai bine better
mai m May
mai mult more
mai putin less
mai putin repede; mai încet; mai rar slow(ly)
mai rău worse
mâine tomorrow
maiou nt undershirt
maiou nt vest (Br.)

mamă f mother
mână f hand
mânăstire f abbey
mânăstire f convent
mânăstire f monastery
mâncare f dish
mâncare f food
mâncăruri fpl cuisine
mandarină f tangerine
mandat nt money order
mânecă f sleeve
manichiură f manicure
mănușă f glove
măr nt apple
mărar nt dill
mare big
mare large
mare f sea
Marea Britanie f Great Britain
mărime f size
marinat(ă) marinated
marmeladă fmarmalade
maro brown
marti f Tuesday
martie m March
masă f meal
masă f table
masă f pliantă folding table
masaj nt message
mască f face pack
măslin m olive
măsură f shape
măsură f size (clothes, shoes)
mat matt (finish)
mătase f silk
material nt material (cloth)
material nt flaușat toweling (terrycloth)
matineu nt matinée
mătușă f aunt
maxilar nt jaw
mazăre f pea
meșa f wick
mecanic m mechanic
mecanic m auto car mechanic
meci nt match (sport)
medic m **oculist** eye specialist
medicină f; (drug) medicament nt medicine
meniu nt menu

meniu nt fix set menu
mentă f mint
mersul nt trenurilor timetable (trains)
metrou nt subway (railway)
metrou nt underground (railway)
metru m metre
mic low
mic small
micul dejun nt breakfast
miel m lamb (meat)
miercuri f Wednesday
miere f honey
miezul noptii nt midnight
migdală f almond
mijloace ntpl de transport transport,
    means of
mijloc middle
miliard nt milliard
milion nt million
miljoace npl means
minge f ball (inflated)
minge f de plajă beach ball
minunat enjoyable
minunat wonderful
minut nt minute
miop short-sighted
mirodenii fpl herbs
mobilă f stil furniture
mocasini mpl moccasin
model nt pattern
moment nt moment
monument nt monument
monument nt comemorativ memorial
morcov m carrot
mormânt nt tomb
moschee f mosque
motel nt motel
motocicletă f motorbike
motor nt engine (car)
motoretă m moped
motorină f diesel
muşchi m muscle
muştar nt mustard
mult lot (a lot)
mult much
multi m, multe f many
mulţumesc thank you
munte m mountain

mură f blackberry
mustată f moustache
muzeu nt museum
muzică f music
muzică f de cameră chamber music
muzică f populară folk music

N

naştere f birth
nap m turnip
nas nt nose
născut born
nasture m button
nationalitate f nationality
natural natural
navă f cu aripi portante hydrofoil
navigatie f sailing
neşifonat wrinkle-free
nealcoolic non-alcoholic
necăsătorit single (unmarried)
nefumător m nonsmoker
negativ nt negative
negru black
nemaipomenit tremendous
nemultumit dissatisfied
nepoată f niece
nepot m nephew
nerv m nerve
nişte some
nici un any
niciodată never
niciunul m; niciuna f none
nimic nothing
nisip nt sand
noapte bună good night
noapte f night
noembrie m November
noi we
nor m cloud
nord nt north
normal normal
noroc nt cheers!
noroc nt luck
Norvegia f Norway
nota f de plată check (restaurant)
nota f de plată; (banknote) bancnotă f bill
nou new
nouă nine
Noua Zeelandă f New Zealand

nouăsprezece nineteen
nouăzeci ninety
nt de noapte nightclub club
nt telefonic dialing code prefix
nu no
nu not
nu este periculos safe (free from danger)
nu iese la spălat colourfast
nu prea scump inexpensive
nu se șifonează crease resistant
nu-i aici absent
nuc m walnut
nucșoară f nutmeg
nucă de cocos coconut
numai; doar only
număr nt number
număr nt de telefon telephone number
numărul nt camerei room number
nume nt name
numele nt de familie last name
numele nt de familie surname
numismatica f coins

O

o dată once
o mie f thousand
o sută hundred
oală f de noapte bedpan
oameni mpl people
obiect nt article
obiectiv nt lens (camera)
obiectiv nt superangular wide-angle lens
obiectiv nt turistic important point of interest (sight)
oblon nt; (camera) obturator nt shutter (window)
obosit tired
ochelari npl glasses
ochelari ntpl de soare sunglasses
ochi m eye
octombrie m October
ocupat busy
ocupat engaged (phone)
ocupat occupied
ocupația f occupation (profession)
ocupație f profession (occupation)
oglindă f mirror
ojă f de unghii nail polish
Olanda f Netherlands

olărit nt pottery
onix nt onyx
operă f opera
operă f opera house
operație f operation
operator telefonist(ă) m/f switchboard
oprește! stop!
opt eight
optician m optician
optsprezece eighteen
optzeci eighty
oră f hour
oră f o'clock
oră f time
oră f; zi f time (occasion)
oraș nt city
oraș nt town
oraș nt vechi old town
orașul nt home town
orchestră f orchestra
orele fpl de vizită visiting hours
orez nt rice
ornitologie f ornithology
os nt bone
ospătar m șef head waiter
oțet nt vinegar
otravă f poison
ou fiert nt boiled egg
ou n (fiert) tare hard-boiled (egg)
ou nt egg
ou nt prăjit fried egg
oval oval

P

pașaport nt passport
Paște m Easter
pachet nt packet
pacient m patient
pădure f forest
pădure f wood
pahar nt glass
pahar nt tumbler
pâine f bread
pâine f prăjită toast
paisprezece fourteen
pajiște f meadow
pălărie f hat
palat nt palace
paletă f de culori color chart

palier nt floor
palpitatii fpl palpitations
pămătuf nt de ras shaving brush
până until
pană f breakdown
pană f de cauciuc puncture (flat tyre)
până la to
pandantiv m pendant
panglică f ribbon
pansamente ntpl Band-Aid®
pantaloni mpl pants (trousers)
pantaloni mpl trousers
pantof m shoe
pantofi mpl de tenis sneaker
pantofi mpl plati (fără toc) flat (shoe)
pânzeturi fpl fabric (cloth)
papetărie f stationer's
papion nt bow tie
păpuşă f doll
papuc m slipper
par avion airmail
păr nt hair
păr nt de cămilă camel-hair
pară f pear
parafină f paraffin (fuel)
parbriz nt windscreen/shield
parc nt park
parcare f car park
parcare f parking
parcare f parking lot
pardon excuse me
parfum nt perfume
parfumerie f toiletry
părinţi mpl parents
parte f side
particular private
pasăre f bird
pasăre f fowl
păsări fpl poultry
pastă de dinţi f toothpaste
pastile fpl pentru dureri de gât throat lozenge
pastor m minister (religion)
păstrăv m trout
pat de camping nt campbed
pat nt bed
pat nt dublu double bed
pată f stain

patină f skate
patine fpl cu rotile roller skate
patinoar nt skating rink
pătrat nt; (town) piaţă f square
patru four
pătrunjel m parsley
patruzeci forty
pătură f blanket
pătut nt cot
peon
pe jos on foot
pe noapte per night
pe oră per hour
pe săptămână per week
pe undeva anywhere
pe zi per day
peşte m fish
peşteră f cave
peisaj nt landscape
peisaj nt scenery
penicilină f penicillin
pensetă f tweezers
pensionar m pensioner
pensiune f completă American plan
pensiune f completă full board
pentru for
pepene m galben melon
pepene m roşu water melon
perciuni mpl sideboards/-burns
perdea f curtain
pereche f pair
pericol nt danger
periculos dangerous
perie f de dinţi toothbrush
perie f de păr hairbrush
periuţă f de unghii nail brush
perlă f pearl
permanent nt permanent wave
permis nt permit
pernă f pillow
peron nt platform (station)
persoană f person
persoane fpl invalide disabled
personal personal
personal nt staff (personnel)
perucă f wig
pescărie f fishmonger's
petrecere f party (social gathering)

piață f market
piatră f prețioasă gem
picătură f drop (liquid)
picături de nas fpl nose drops
picături fpl de ochi eye drops
picături fpl de tuse cough drops
picior nt leg
pick-up nt record player
picnic nt picnic
pictor m painter
pictură f; tablou nt painting
piele f leather
piele f skin
piele f de căprioară suede
piept nt chest
piept nt de găină chicken breast
pieptene m comb
pierdere f loss
piersică f peach
piesă f play (theatre)
pieton m pedestrian
pijama f nightdress/-gown
pijama f pyjamas
pilă f emery board
pilă f de unghii nail file
pioneză f thumbtack
pioneze fpl drawing pins
pipă f pipe
piper m pepper
piscină f swimming pool
pistă f ski run
pix nt cu pastă ball-point pen
plăcintărie f pastry shop
plajă f beach
plămân nt lung
planetar m planetarium
plasă f contra tănțarilor mosquito net
plastic plastic
plată f fee (doctor's)
plată f payment
plated argintat silver
platină f platinum
pleacă de aici go away!
plecări fpl departure
plic nt envelope
plin full
ploaie f rain
plombă f filling (tooth)

plumb nt lead (metal)
pneumonie f pneumonia
poșta f mail
poșta f post office
poșta f post (mail)
poate perhaps
pod nt bridge
poftim/poftiți pardon, I beg your
pojar nt measles
poliție f police
pompă f pump
poplin nt poplin
porc m pig
porc m pork
porc m mistreț wild boar
port nt harbour
port nt port
port-aparat nt camera case
port-aparat nt case
port-ochelari nt spectacle case
port-țigaret nt cigarette holder
portabil portable
porție f portion
portmoneu nt wallet
portocală f orange (fruit)
portocaliu orange (colour)
Portugalia f Portugal
porumb nt corn (sweet)
porumbel m pigeon
post nt de poliție; centru nt de poliție police station
post restant nt general delivery
potârniche f partridge
potecă f footpath
potecă f path
poză f picture (photo)
poză f print (photo)
poză f; fotografie f photo
prăjină f pole (ski)
prăjit fried
prăjit roasted
prăjitură f cake
praz nt leeks
prea mult too much
prea prăjită overdone (meat)
prefix nt area code
prelungitor nt extension cord/lead
prenume nt first name

preot m priest
prepeliță f quail
preservativ m condom
presiune f; **tensiune** f pressure
preț nt; **cost** nt cost
preț nt; **cost** nt; **tarif** nt price
prevedere f forecast
prezbit m long-sighted
prezentare f introduction (social)
prieten m boyfriend
prieten m friend
prietenă f girlfriend
primărie f town hall
primăvară f spring (season)
primul first
prin through
priză f outlet (electric)
priză f socket (electric)
procent nt per cent
procentaj nt percentage
profit nt profit
program nt programme
programare f; **întâlnire** f appointment
pronunție f pronunciation
propoziție f sentence
prosop nt towel
prosop nt de baie bath towel
protestant m Protestant
proteză f denture
provizoriu temporary
prună f plum
prune fpl uscate prune
pudră f powder
pudră f compactă powder compact
pudră f de obraz face powder
pudră f de talc talcum powder
puf nt de pudră powder puff
pui m chicken
pulovăr nt pullover
pulover nt jumper
pulover nt sweater
pulover nt cu guler în jurul gâtului
    round-neck
pulover nt cu guler pe gât roll-neck
punct nt de îmbarcare embarkation point
pungă f cu cuburi de gheață ice pack
pungă f de plastic plastic bag
punte f deck (ship)

pur pure
puțin little (a little)
puțini; (a few) câțiva few

R

rabin m rabbi
rac m crayfish (river)
răceală f; **gripă** f cold (illness)
rachetă f racket (sport)
rachetă f de tenis tennis racket
radiator nt radiator (car)
radio nt radio
radio nt de mașină car radio
radio-ceas nt alarm clock
radio-ceas nt clock-radio
radiografie f X-ray
raft nt shelf
raion nt section
raliu nt car racing
ramă f frame (glasses)
rană f injury
rană f wound
rănit injured
rapid (tren) nt fast
ras nt shave
răspuns nt answer
rață f duck
rată f rate (inflation)
rata f inflației inflation rate
rătăcit lost
rău bad
râu nt river
rău nt de altitudine altitude sickness
rău nt de călătorie travel sickness
rece; frig cold
recepție f reception
recepționist m receptionist
reclamație f complaint
recoltare f specimen (medical)
rectangular(ă) rectangular
reduce f reduction
reducere f discount
regim n alimentar diet
regizor m director (theatre)
religie f religion
remover acetonă f nail polish
repede quick(ly)
Republica Cehă f Czech Republic
rest nt rest

restaurant nt restaurant
restituire f withdrawal
reţetă f prescription
reumatism nt rheumatism
revistă f magazine
rezervă f de stilou refill (pen)
rezervare f la hotel hotel reservation
rezervat reserved
rezervaţie f reservation
ridiche f radish
rinichi mpl kidney
roşie f tomato
roşu-aprins; stacojiu scarlet
roşu-închis, purpuriu purple
roşu; wine vin nt roşu red
roată f tire (tyre)
roată f wheel
roată f de rezervă spare tyre
robinet nt faucet
rochie f dress
rol nt principal lead (theatre)
rom nt rum
româneşte Romanian (language)
România f Romania
rotund round
roz pink
rozariu nt rosary
rozmarin m rosemary
rubin nt ruby
rucsac nt backpack
rucsac nt rucksack
rufe fpl de spălat laundry (clothes)
ruină f ruin
ruj nt rouge
ruj nt de buze lipstick
ruj nt de obraz blusher
rulotă f caravan
rulotă f trailer
rupt torn
Rusia f Russia

S

sac m de voiaj traveling bag
sac m; pungă f bag
sac nt de dormit sleeping bag
safir nt sapphire
sală de concert f concert hall
sala f de aşteptare waiting room
sală f de conferinţe conference room

salamuri npl cold cuts
salată f salad
salată f de fructe fruit salad
salată f verde lettuce
salon nt de cosmetică beauty salon
salopete fpl overalls
saltea f mattress
saltea f de burete de cauciuc foam rubber mattress
saltea f pneumatică air bed
saltea f pneumatică air mattress
salut nt greeting
salutări fpl regards
salvamar m life guard (beach)
salvare f ambulance
salvie f sage
sâmbătă f Saturday
sân m breast
sandale fpl sandals
sânge nt blood
sângera bleed, to a
săptămână f week
săpun nt soap
sărat salty
sărbătoare f legală public holiday
sardele fpl sardines
sare f salt
săruri de baie fpl bath salts
sat nt village
satin nt satin
sau or
scaun nt chair
scaun nt stools
scaun nt pliant folding chair
schi nautic water-skis
schi nt ski
schi nt skiing
schimb nt currency
scoci nt adhesive tape
scop de serviciu nt business trip
scorţişoară f cinnamon
Scoţia f Scotland
scrisoare f letter
scrisoare f acreditivă letter of credit
scrob nt scrambled eggs
scrumieră f ashtray
scule fpl tools
sculptor m sculptor

sculptură f sculpture
scump expensive
scurt short
scutec nt nappy
scutec nt **de unică folosință** diaper
scuter nt scooter
scuzati; regret sorry
se întoarce back, to be/to get a
se spală washable care
seară f evening
secol nt century
secretară f secretary
secundar nt second hand (watch)
seif n safe
sejur nt stay
semafor nt traffic light
semn nt **de circulatie** road sign
semne ntpl signs (notice)
sendvici nt; **sandviş** nt sandwich
sens unic nt one-way (traffic)
separat separately
septembrie m September
servicii ntpl **de spălătorie** laundry service
serviciu nt service
serviciu nt **de cameră** room service
sfârşit nt end
sfârşit nt **de săptămână** weekend
sfeclă f **roşie** beetroot
sfert nt quarter
sfert nt **de oră** quarter of an hour
sfoară f string
sigur certain
simplă plain (colour)
simplu simple
sinagogă f synagogue
sintetic synthetic
sistem nt system
slab mild (light)
Slovacia f Slovakia
slujbă f **religioasă** mass (church)
slujbă f **religioasă** religious service
slujbă f **religioasă** service (church)
smarald nt emerald
smochină f fig
soare m sun
solduri ntpl; **(commerce) vânzare** f sale (bargains)
solist m soloist
somnifer nt pill

somnifer nt sleeping pill
sonerie f bell (electric)
soră (medicală) f nurse
soră f sister
sos nt sauce
sosiri fpl arrival
soţ m husband
sotie f wife
sovârv m oregano
spălătorie f laundry (place)
spălătorie f **Nufărul** launderette
spanac nt spinach
Spania f Spain
sparanghel m asparagus
spart, rupt broken defect;
spate nt back
spatiu nt room (space)
special special
specialist m specialist
specialitate f speciality
spectacol nt show
spectacol nt **în mijlocul publicului** floor show
spital nt hospital
sport nt sport
sporturi ntpl **de iarnă** winter sports
spray nt **contra insectelor** insect repellent
spre towards
spumă f **de baie** bubble bath
spune; a comanda ask for, to a
stadion nt stadium
stafidă f raisin
stafide fpl currants
stal nt orchestra (seats)
stal nt stalls (theatre)
stâlp m **de cort** pole (tent)
stâlp m **de cort** tent pole
stâncă f cliff
stânga left
Statele Unite fpl United States
staţie f **de autobuz** bus stop
staţie f **de autobuz** stop (bus)
staţie f **de benzină** filling station
staţie f **de metrou; (metrou)** nt metro station (underground, subway)
staţie de taxi taxi rank/stand
staţie facultativă on request
staţie facultativă request
statuie f statue

stea f star
sticlă f bottle
sticlă f şlefuită cut glass
stilou nt pen
stilou nt cu cerneală fountain pen
stoc nt terminat out of stock
stomac nt stomach
stomacul nt deranjat upset stomach (**a avea**)
stradă f street
strâmt narrow
strâmt tight (close-fitting)
straniu strange
strugurel nt de buze lipsalve
struguri mplgrapes
student m student
sturion m sturgeon
sub under
subtire thin
suc nt juice
suc nt de fructe fruit juice
suc nt de grepfrut grapefruit juice
suc nt de portocale orange juice
suc nt de roşii tomato juice
sud nt south
Suedia f Sweden
sufragerie; sala de mese f dining room
sumă f amount
sumbru gloomy
supă f soup
super super (petrol)
superb superb
supozitoare ntpl suppository
sus up
sutien nt bra
suvenir nt souvenir
suzetă f dummy (baby's)
suzetă f pacifier (baby's)

T

tabacheră f cigarette case
tabletă f tablet (medical)
tablou nt picture (painting)
tacâmuri ntpl cutlery
tăietură f cut (wound)
tăiţei mpl noodles
talcioc nt flea market
talisman nt charm (trinket)
talpă f sole (shoe)
tampon nt extern sanitary napkin/towel

tampon nt intern tampon
tampon nt pentru demachiat make-up
  remover pad
tapiserie f tapestry
ţară f country
tare; puternic strong
târg nt fair
tarhon m tarragon
tarif nt arrangement (set price)
tartă f tart
târziu late
tată m father
taxă f pe valoare adăugată value-added ta
taxă f; TVA tax
taxă turistică f tourist tax
taxi nt taxi
teatru nt theatre
teavă f de eşapament exhaust pipe
teleferic nt cable car
telefon nt telephone
telefon nt telephone booth
telegramă f telegram
telemetru nt rangefinder
teleobiectiv nt telephoto lens
teleschi nt ski lift
televizor nt television
telex nt telex
ţelină f celery
temperatură f temperature
tendon nt tendon
tenişi mpl plimsolls
tenis nt tennis
tensiune f arterială; puls nt blood pressure
terasă f terrace
teren nt de golf golf course
teren nt de joc playground
teren nt de tenis tennis court
termen m term (word)
termometru nt thermometer
termos nt vacuum flask
termos nt water flask
tetanus nt tetanus
the seara evening, in
tifon nt gauze
tigaie f frying pan
ţigară f cigarette
ţigări fpl mentolate menthol (cigarettes)
timbru nt postage stamp
timbru nt stamp (postage)

tînăr m young
ţinută obligatorie f; (woman's) **rochie de seară** f evening dress
ţipar m eel
tirbuşon nt corkscrew
toaleta f toilets
toamnă f autumn
toamnă f fall (autumn)
toc nt heel
tocană f stew
tot all
tot, toate everything
trabuc nt cigar
trafic nt traffic
tramvai nt streetcar
tramvai nt tram
tranchilizant nt tranquillizer
transfer nt transfer (finance)
transformator nt transformer
transfuzie f **de sânge** blood transfusion
Transilvania f Transylvania
traseu nt route
traseu nt sightseeing tour
traseu nt **turistic (spre)** scenic route
tratament nt treatment
traversare f crossing (maritime)
trecătoare f pass (mountain)
trei three
treisprezece thirteen
treizeci thirty
tren nt train
tren nt direct through train
trening nt tracksuit
tribunal nt court house
trusă f **de prim ajutor** first-aid kit
tu, dumneavoastră you
tub nt tube
tub nt **de scafandru** snorkel
ţuică f brandy
tunet nt thunder
tunsoare f haircut
Turcia f Turkey
turcoaz; colour turcoaz turquoise
turn nt tower
tuse f cough
tutun nt tobacco
tutun nt **de mestecat** chewing tobacco
tutun nt **de pipă** pipe tobacco
tutun nt **de prizat** snuff

tutungerie f tobacconist's
tyre roată f **dezumflată** flat

U

uşor easy
uşor; (colour) deschis light
Ucraina f Ukraine
ulei nt oil
ulei nt **de bronzat** sun-tan oil
ultimul; trecut last
uluitor amazing
umăr m shoulder
umbrelă f umbrella
umbrelă f **de soare** umbrella (beach)
umeraş nt hanger
umflat swollen
umflătură f bump (lump)
umflătură f lump (bump)
umflătură f swelling
umplut stuffed
un (bilet) dus nt one-way ticket
un dus single (ticket)
un pieptănat nt blow-dry
unchi m uncle
unde where
undeva somewhere
unelte ntpl **de pescuit** fishing tackle
unghie f nail (human)
universitate f university
unsprezece eleven
unt nt butter
unu one
urare f wish
urât ugly
ureche f ear
urgent urgent
urgenţă f emergency
urină f urine
următorul; viitor next
uscat; sec dry
uscător nt **de păr** hair dryer
usturoi m garlic
util useful
uzina f factory
uzuale; general general

V

vă rog please
vacă f beef

vacanță f holiday
vacanță f vacation
vacanță; concediu nt holidays
vagon nt **de dormit** sleeping car
vagon restaurant nt dining car
val nt wave
vale f valley
valet m hall porter
valiză f suitcase
valoare f value
vamă f customs
vamă f duty (customs)
vânat game (food)
vânătă f aubergine
vânătă f eggplant
vânătaie f bruise
vânătoare f hunting
vanilie f vanilla
vânt nt wind
vapor nt ship
văr m cousin
vară f summer
vârf (în vârful capului); sus top, at the
vârf nt peak
vârstă f age
varză f cabbage
varză f acră sauerkraut
varză f de Bruxelles Brussels sprouts
vată f absorbent cotton
vată f cotton wool
vechi, bătrânold
vedere f eyesight
vedere f postcard
vedere f view (panorama)
vegetarian vegetarian
velur nt corduroy
venă f vein
verde green
verighetă f wedding ring
veritabil real (genuine)
vermut nt vermouth
veselă f crockery
vest nt west
vestă f vest (Am.)

vestă f waistcoat
veterinar m veterinarian
vezică f urinară bladder
vie f vineyard
vin nt wine
vineri f Friday
vis-a-vis opposite
vitamine (tablete) fpl vitamin pill
vitel m veal
viteză f speed
vitrină f shop window
vizită f visit
vodcă f vodka
volei nt volleyball
voltaj nt voltage
vopsea f dye
vopsea f paint
vopsea f tint
vreme f weather
vreo, cam about (approximately)

W

whisky nt whisky
winder maneta f de rulat filmul film
windsurfer m windsurfer

Z

zahăr nt sugar
zaharină f sweetener
zăpadă f snow
zbor nt flight
zece ten
zero zero
zgomotos noisy
zi f day
zi f de naștere birthday
zi f lucrătoare weekday
zi f lucrătoare working day
zi liberă f day off
ziar nt newspaper
zid nt wall
zmeură f raspberry
zona f băncilor business district
zoologie f zoology